The Long Mynd: Its History and Wildlife

In association with the National Trust

The Long Mynd: Its History and Wildlife

Published by Greengates Publications,
69 High Street, Church Stretton, Shropshire, SY6 6BY.

A catalogue record for this book is available from the British Library.

ISBN 978-0-9568018-1-4

Printed by Cambrian Printers, Aberystwyth

The Long Mynd

Its History and Wildlife

Barrie Raynor

To
Ellen, Anna, Alasdair and Finlay

Every once in a while we all need to get out, to give ourselves up to a favourite wild landscape, to explore and experience and to wonder. We should do this in every season and all weathers, by day and by night. We should touch and smell and listen. We should absorb moonlight on water, feel the wind in our hair, and discover the other creatures with which we share the world. We should be forcing ourselves to reconnect with wild nature and our origins. We need to do this before it's too late.

Jeff Watson, scientist and conservationist [1952-2007] in J Lister Kaye, *At the Water's Edge*

Acknowledgements

In writing this book, I am particularly indebted to the staff of the National Trust Carding Mill Valley office who have given me so much of their time in answering my questions, supplying me with numerous reports and research material and allowing me to use their magnificent collection of photographs. My thanks are due particularly to Peter Carty, David Cowell, Chris Stratton and Caroline Uff who between them have read early drafts of the book and made many corrections and suggestions. Without them and the help they have provided, the book could not have been written.

I particularly thank the generosity of the many photographers who have allowed me to use their beautiful photographs without which this would be a very dull book, in particular local photographers Robin Jukes-Hughes, Pete and Kate Johnson, Andrew and Ann Middleton, Yvonne Beaumont, Paul Miller and the late Richard Warren. I apologise if there have been any photographs wrongly attributed in the text. In addition to the photographs from the National Trust Shropshire Hills' collection, other photographs have been obtained through the Creative Commons Licencing organisation, North East Wildlife and from Tony Crowe's collection of historic photographs of Church Stretton to whom my thanks are due.

I have had valuable discussions with Tony Crowe, Peter Toghill, Ian Dormor, Leo Smith, Peter Aspinall, Richard Hickman, Hilary Jones, Alan Brisbourne, Malcolm Loft and Merle Wilson whose special expertise on a variety of topics has added considerably to the fund of information I have been able to use in compiling this book.

Last, but by no means least, I am grateful to Richard Bonfield for allowing me to reprint three of his 'seasonal' poems originally published in his compilations *Animated Nature* and *Swan for all Seasons*.

The most useful research sources used were:

Leo Smith, Peter Carty and Caroline Uff, *Wild Mynd: Birds and Wildlife of the Long Mynd*, Hobby Publications, 2007.

National Trust Nature Conservation Evaluation, Long Mynd, Shropshire, 2008.

Robert Woodside and Jeremy Milln, *National Trust Archaeological Survey, The Long Mynd*, 1995.

The Victoria County History of Shropshire, vol. 10 (1998).

The Long Mynd: its Ecology, Past, Present and Future. Proceedings of a Symposium at the University of Wolverhampton, 2003.

Kate Thorne, *The Story of the Long Mynd told through its rights of way*, 1994.

Photos © Barrie Raynor, Hilary Chambers, Richard Warren and Robin Jukes-Hughes

Contents

Into my heart an air that kills
From yon far country blows:
What are those blue remembered hills,
What spires, what farms are those?

That is the land of lost content,
I see it shining plain,
The happy highways where I went
And cannot come again.

A E Housman

Photos © NT Shropshire Hills, Barrie Raynor,
Robin Jukes-Hughes, Chris Stratton

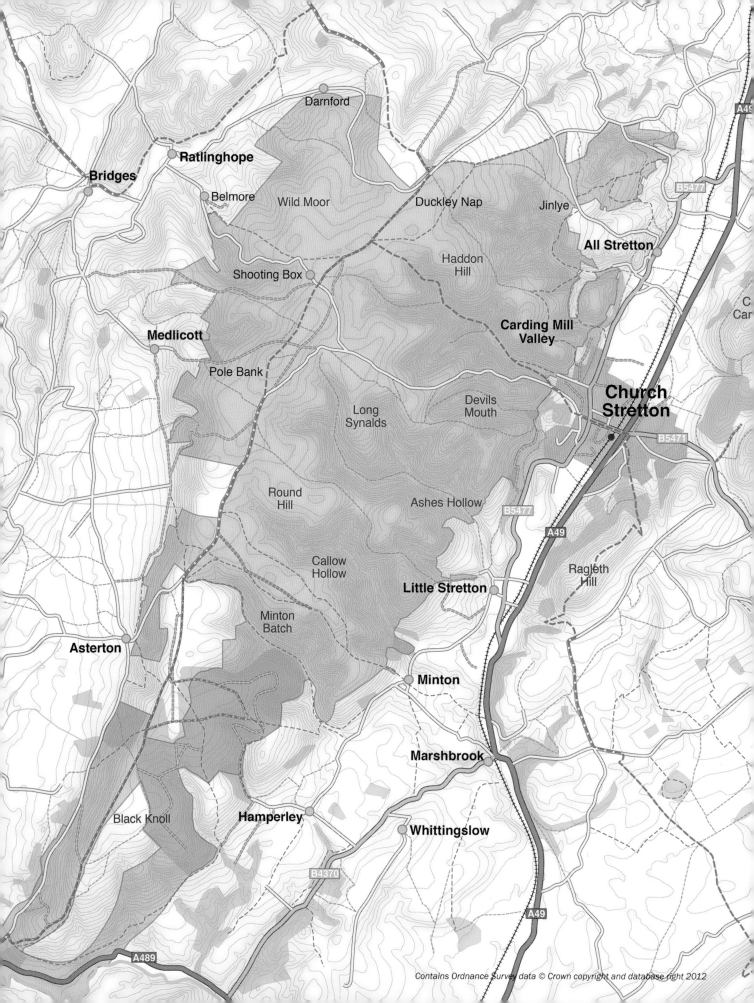

The Long Mynd

SITUATED in the midst of the rolling South Shropshire countryside, the Long Mynd is a dramatic, isolated, whaleback hill with an open expanse of heathland and deeply cut valleys, particularly on the eastern side (see the photograph below). In contrast, the western side of the hill is terminated by a steep scarp slope with fewer valleys. The valleys, or batches which are their local name, contain tumbling streams and waterfalls. The plateau is dominated by heather and is exposed and windswept with mires and flushes where the streams rise, providing a habitat for a diverse flora and fauna. The abundance of heather declines towards the margins of the plateau giving rise to bilberry, bracken and open grassland.

The Long Mynd has a landscape with an important geology and an interesting archaeology which records the presence of human activity over thousands of years. The area was never covered with dense forest so it was relatively easy for prehistoric man to clear and use. However, the thin soils, exposed conditions and inhospitable nature determined the vegetation and types of farming, leading to mainly seasonal pastoral usage. Apart from the Bodbury Ring hill fort, human settlements were at lower altitude in the sheltered valleys where the alluvial soils provided good grazing for their stock.

The Long Mynd is within the Shropshire Hills Area of Outstanding Natural Beauty (AONB) and is a site of biological and geological special scientific interest (SSSI). The National Trust owns 2,322 hectares (5,737 acres), about half of it. The Long Mynd stretches about 11 km (7 miles) from north to south and about 8 km (5 miles) at its widest point in the north and about 2 km (1 mile) wide at its highest southern point, Black Knoll. The highest point of the Long Mynd is 516 m (1,693 ft) above sea level at Pole Bank[1]. Almost all of the plateau area is above 400 m. In all directions there are spectacular views with the Stiperstones, Berwyns and Cadair Idris to the west, Clee Hills and the Malverns to the east, The Wrekin and the Staffordshire hills to the north, and the Black Mountains to the south.

Whilst the south, west and east boundaries of the Long Mynd are reasonably clear, to the north, the hill becomes progressively lower. The northern boundary of heathland is around High Park and Womerton and though the rock formations which characterise the Long Mynd continue northwards they only show occasionally as outcrops such as at Lyth Hill, at Sharpstone (Bayston Hill) where there is an important quarry for road stone, and Haughmond Hill.

The name Long Mynd simply means 'long hill' from the Old English *lang* (long) and the Welsh *mynydd* (hill), referring to the dominant profile of the hill. Its name was first recorded in 1175.

The Long Mynd from Caer Caradoc

The Shaping of the Long Mynd

THE LONG MYND stands as an island between the Stiperstones to the west and Caradoc, Helmeth, Hazler and Ragleth Hills to the east. It differs from these hills by being flat-topped and having deep valleys cutting into its side. On closer inspection its vegetation and topography is also different. Why is this?

Origins: the First Rocks

The hills on either side of the Church Stretton valley have a history going back over 570 million years to when the rocks which form these hills were first formed. At that time the land mass of the continents which we know today were all clumped together in the southern hemisphere. Over huge periods of time, these land masses, called plates, moved over the surface of the planet separating from each other, breaking apart or bumping into each other. This movement was driven by enormously violent earthquakes and volcanic eruptions of lava which created fresh crust which pushed the continental plates apart. The movement of these continental plates is still happening today, for example the North American continent is moving away from Europe at the rate of 2 cm each year. This concept called plate tectonics explains how continents move about the earth's surface as well as explaining the rôle of volcanoes in mountain building which is associated with plate boundaries.

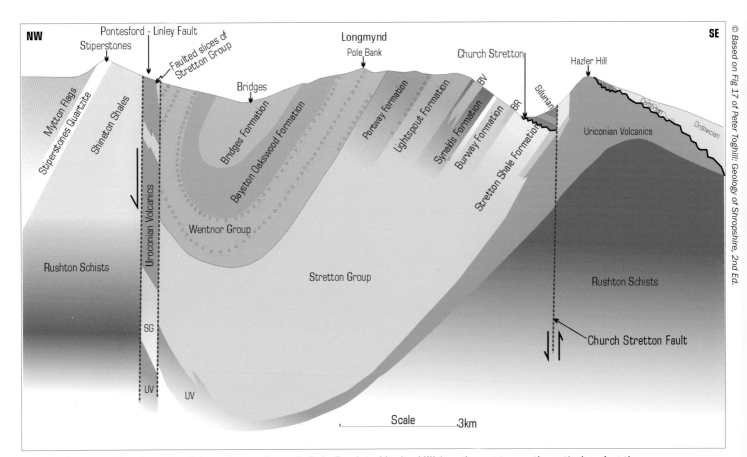

© Based on Fig 17 of Peter Toghill: Geology of Shropshire, 2nd Ed.

Cross section from the Stiperstones, through Pole Bank to Hazler Hill (northwest to southeast) showing the principal geological formations which give rise to the Long Mynd, in particular the giant downfold (syncline). BR is Buxton Rock, BV is Batch Volcanics. The Church Stretton fault is shown. The smaller fault giving rise to the scarp slope on the west side of the Long Mynd does not appear on this cross section but would do so on a cross section 5 miles to the south.

Volcanoes, Lava and Ash

570–560 million years ago, during what is known as the Precambrian period, the Shropshire area we know today lay on the edge of a huge land mass close to the Antarctic Circle at around 60° south of the equator, well south of where Cape Horn is today. Here, one plate was being pushed against and rode over another plate causing intense volcanic activity where they met. These volcanoes poured out huge quantities of lava and ash which ultimately formed the Stretton Hills on the eastern side of the Church Stretton valley including Caer Caradoc, Ragleth Hill and The Lawley as well as The Wrekin and also spread far to the west. The amount of lava and ash eventually reached a thickness of some 4 km.

The volcanoes were probably tens of kilometres away to the east from where Church Stretton now stands. Although Caer Caradoc and The Wrekin look like extinct volcanoes, they are not; they are the remnants of mounds of volcanic lava and ash. In fact, outcrops of this lava on the summit ridge of Caer Caradoc still have the gas bubble holes preserved which were caused by the escaping dissolved gasses in the molten lava. At that time the landscape was barren with no life on land and only bacteria, algae and some primitive jellyfish in the sea.

Accompanying this tectonic plate movement, prolonged volcanic activity and violent earthquakes caused the earth's brittle crust to split further creating long lines of deep cracks called faults. One of these, the famous Church Stretton fault stretches all the way from Staffordshire to South Wales running along the east side of the Church Stretton valley and through the Marshbrook to Horderley gap. It was a lateral shift whereby the west side moved southwards tens of kilometres over many millennia relative to the east side in a manner similar to the movement of the San Andreas fault in California. Much later, only 50 million years ago, the west side of the fault catastrophically dropped about 1,100 m relative to the east side.

A smaller fault on the west side of the Long Mynd formed about 400 million years ago gives rise to the spectacular 200 m high west-facing scarp slope. The site of the Gliding Club is close by and the up draught of warm air at the scarp edge also makes it a favourite site for the launch of hang gliders.

Covered by the Sea

At the same time as the volcanoes were erupting, the continuously violent weather was wearing away the mountains which had been formed. Tumbling rivers took the eroded rock, boulders and sand down to the sea which by now had encroached over the area to the west of the Church Stretton fault. The eroded material was laid down as layers of sediment on the sea floor and nearby coastline. Thick inter-tidal muds and silts accumulated on these sediments, dried out and were compressed by burial under more sediment to form the layered sedimentary rocks such as sandstones, shales, mud stones and conglomerates which comprise the Long Mynd today. Eventually an enormous thickness of sediment accumulated, estimated at about 7,000 m deep.

The Church Stretton fault lies at the foot of Caer Caradoc at the boundary (red arrows) between the green pastures on good soil (later created from glacial till) and the trees growing on the poor volcanic sub-soil. Farmers readily recognised the change in soil types. Further south, the fault line runs along Watling Street North (behind Coppice Leasowes) and Watling Street South and then along the A49. This is a straight line when seen from the air.

In these sedimentary layers on the Long Mynd there are fossilised bacteria, the soft-bodied *Beltanelliformis minutae*, which appear as ellipsoidal structures about 1.5–2.0 mm diameter. These rare and unusual fossils have been dated at 555.9±3.5 million years ago. They are causing a lot of interest among the scientific community because they are amongst the oldest fossils known.

Around 560 million years ago the sedimentary and volcanic rocks to the west of the Stretton Hills were affected by great sideways forces as tectonic plates came together. The rocks were squeezed, resulting in a giant downward fold called a syncline, about 10 km across (see diagram on page 2). The steeply inclined layers of sedimentary rock within the fold structure are almost vertical and can be seen today in the sides of the main valleys of the Long Mynd.

Near vertical strata exposed on the side of The Burway.

The scarp slope on the west edge of the Long Mynd. Photo taken from a hang glider, looking south.

A Tropical Land

Over subsequent millions of years, the tectonic plate on which Shropshire and southern Britain stood moved slowly north from the Antarctic Circle at the rate of about 5 cm per year, through equatorial regions, to our present northern latitudes which it reached about 60 million years ago. Throughout the intervening time, considerable deposition of more sediment took place as well as erosion by weathering. As the land mass of Britain was pushed northwards through the tropics, the flora and fauna were affected by the climate as it changed from sub-tropical to tropical and to the temperate climate of today.

By this time, the whole of Britain had been uplifted and emerged as a land surface on which the modern river patterns and coast lines would develop. Since then, an enormous amount of weathering by wind, rain, frost and ice has taken place to remove much of the sedimentary rock which had covered the Long Mynd area since Precambrian times. Eventually the Long Mynd and Stretton Hills began to appear around 30 million years ago with their characteristic modern shapes along with the Church Stretton valley which developed as we see it today after this erosion.

Ice Ages

From about 2.4 million years ago Britain and most of the northern hemisphere was gripped by ice. From that date great ice sheets and glaciers covered Wales and the Midlands as far south as the Thames valley. Since then, there were probably over twenty advances and retreats of ice sheets from the north with warmer periods in between. Little is known about the earlier ice ages over Shropshire other than they certainly covered the Long Mynd and the Stretton Hills. Unfortunately most of the evidence for them has been wiped out by subsequent glacial action from the most recent ice age.

There is, however, a great deal of evidence in Shropshire and around the Long Mynd of the last glacial period when an ice sheet spread from the Irish Sea across the Cheshire plain and North Shropshire and southwards into the Church Stretton valley as far south as Marshbrook. At its thickest about 23,000 to 18,000 years ago, the level of this glacial ice reached about 260 m (850 ft) above present sea level and therefore the highest parts of the Long Mynd and the Stretton Hills protruded above the surrounding ice sheets. In fact the ice sheet reached to the top of Sandford Avenue on the road to Hope Bowdler. The top of the Long Mynd and other local hills were subjected to an intense tundra climate and permafrost almost certainly covered the highest parts of the hills. The average temperature would have been about 10 °C lower than experienced now.

The initial formation of the steep valleys on the east side of the Long Mynd probably occurred during the melting of ice in earlier glacial periods over the previous 300,000 years. Thousands of years of tundra freeze-thaw cycles had led to the formation of unstable slopes which quickly eroded away to leave deep V-shaped valleys. Prior to the last ice age, the base of the Church Stretton valley was 30–60 m lower than at present. When the last glacial ice melted and receded northwards, material trapped in the glacier was deposited and raised the valley floor close to its present level.

The reason why there are so many more valleys on the east side of the Long Mynd compared with the west side may be associated with the fact that the plateau tilts slightly to the south-east with the watershed near the western edge thus making melt water drain eastwards. This tilt may be associated with the general tilting of Britain in this direction which occurred about 65 million years ago.

Limit of earlier and latest (blue) ice-sheets.

After the Last Ice Age

When the ice started to melt around 14,000 years ago the large amount of water produced by the melting snow and ice, as well as a very high rainfall, further eroded the valleys on the eastern side of the Long Mynd and the Church Stretton valley itself. As a result of this erosion, large amounts of sand and gravel were washed down from these side valleys into the main Church Stretton valley and added to the sands and clays already left behind by the retreating ice sheet. By 13,000 years ago all the ice had melted leaving the U-shaped Church Stretton valley we have today.

The interlocking smaller valleys on either side of, in particular, Carding Mill valley run in a north-east to south-west direction and follow softer strata. In between these valleys prominent craggy outcrops and ridges such as Pike Ridge, Cow Ridge and Calf Ridge follow the line of much harder strata.

This last ice age accounted for much of the shape of not only the valleys but also the plateau. On the plateau the principal agent of weathering was by frost action which relies on rock fatigue induced by repetitive freeze-thaw cycles, especially during the summer months when the day-time temperature would be above freezing. This process was very effective in breaking up exposed surface rock especially at preexisting lines of weakness at cleavage planes.

The melting of the ice in the batches between Church Stretton and All Stretton left some remarkable overflow (drainage) channels at successive heights on the eastern side of the Long Mynd as the ice sheet thawed. The water flow between the hillside edge and the ice sheet cut out small valleys parallel to the main Church Stretton valley. These are all now dry but can be seen as a series of steps or depressions parallel to the edge of the hill. Good examples are the first fairway of the golf course (below), over the ridge between Cwmdale and The Batch, on Novers Hill, Woodnall and Castle Hill. On the west side of the Long Mynd, good examples are at Myndtown and Myndmill Wood.

The story of how the ancient rocks of the Long Mynd and Stretton Hills were formed allows us to look back into the ancient geological past of over 570 million years to when the world looked very different to how it looks today. The rocks of the Long Mynd, formed as they were during the late Precambrian period, originated before life in abundance appeared on the earth's surface. Fossils are therefore almost absent from the rocks although some fossilised primitive jellyfish, fine filamentous algal mats and bacterial structures have been found.

The first fairway of the Golf Course was once a glacial overflow channel created when the ice melted 14,000 years ago at the end of the last ice age.

The Arrival of Man

Tundra Vegetation

As the last Ice Age drew to a close about 10,000 years ago the Long Mynd was a desolate arctic expanse. As the temperature warmed, the landscape became progressively covered in turn by lichens (arriving as spores in the air), mosses, liverworts and ferns. These pioneers started the formation of basic soils by weathering down the underlying rocks and degrading them. Then followed stunted bushes of birch and willow with ground cover of bilberry and cow berry, the sort of vegetation seen today in the far north of Scandinavia, Russia and Canada.

The Long Mynd probably became covered by birch trees and later by Scots pine with willows in the water-logged valleys. Woodland was continually changing as more species came and were able to establish themselves. Hazel was followed by oak, elm, lime and alder and later by ash and others but as the climate became wetter the pines disappeared. By about 5,000 BC the Long Mynd was thinly covered in trees, predominantly of oak with willows and alders in the boggy valleys.

Mammals Arrive

Until 9,500 years ago, Britain was joined to mainland Europe via a land bridge across the southern end of the North Sea. The land bridge allowed the more mobile species including arctic and tundra specialists such as the arctic fox, Norway lemming, musk ox, mammoth, woolly rhinoceros and reindeer to move into Britain from the rest of Europe as the ice sheet receded.

As the climate became warmer, temperate species such as bear, wolves, beaver, boar, stoats and frogs (but not the less hardy weasels and toads which came later) as well as mankind moved into the new post-glacial woodlands and marshes, gradually expanding their range throughout Britain. Many of these moved further northwards or became extinct (especially reindeer) as their preferred tundra habitat receded and was lost. During this period, man would have hunted the wild deer, oxen, auroch (the wild ancestor of all domestic cattle), pig and wild fowl.

The rise in sea levels caused by the melting of ice from the last ice age resulted in the English Channel breaking through to link up with the North Sea. Once separated from mainland Europe, any loss of animal species whether from hunting or habitat change could not be offset by further immigration. Brown bear, auroch and lynx survived until about 2,000 years ago, whilst wild boar, wolves and beaver clung on until the 16th or 17th century.

The Neolithic Period (3,500 to 2,000 BC)

The Neolithic period (new Stone Age) saw the introduction of agriculture in Britain and the beginning of the gradual reduction of its tree cover. The people of this time, Neolithic farmers, left no evidence of settlement in the Marches although numerous implements of this period made from flint have been found along the Clun–Clee hilltop route. Stone axes were central to the Neolithic economy and provide some evidence for the clearance of land for early agriculture. Axes have been found considerable distances from their source illustrating the ability of Neolithic communities to trade over

© NT Shropshire Hills

Reconstruction of how a flint axe could be held.

© Robin McConnell

© Stefan

© Sharon Mollerus

Among the first mammals to arrive after the ice age were likely to be reindeer, wolves, musk oxen and beavers.

large distances. It has been suggested that an ancient trade route along the Long Mynd existed since a few scattered implements have been found close to it, in particular a polished stone axe-head. Ridgeway and hilltop routes were favoured because the valleys were wooded and boggy and difficult to traverse.

The Bronze Age (2,000 to 700 BC)

With the introduction of metal working about 2,000 BC, stone tools were superseded by ones made of bronze, an alloy of copper and tin. There are over 30 barrows (burial mounds) on the plateau, the highest density in the West Midlands. These indicate that Bronze Age man was here and had a much greater effect on the Long Mynd than their predecessors. These people cleared the remaining oak, birch and willow woodland with their more efficient metal tools so that their animals had grazing and cereals could be planted. It is uncertain how much of the Long Mynd was being farmed or even permanently settled since there is no firm evidence of settlement, cultivation or field systems on the plateau. However, at the far south end of the Long Mynd near Black Knoll, there is clear evidence for a Celtic Iron Age settlement (see page 11).

The barrows were made of earth or stone and originally were surrounded by a circular quarry ditch where the earth is thrown forward to form a rampart. They were very much bigger than the remains seen today and would have required a prodigious amount of time and labour to construct. They are called bowl barrows and each was a burial site for one or occasionally several persons. The burial of the dead on the hill may be because it was a revered place and would have given their ancestors greater proximity to the sky. It does not necessarily mean that Bronze Age man lived permanently on the hill.

The Portway

The Portway is thought to have originated as a prehistoric ridgeway that ran along the open uplands of Shropshire from Plowden to Woolstaston and thence to Shrewsbury avoiding the heavily wooded and wet valleys and minimising river crossings. The traders in Neolithic stone and Bronze Age tools, gold, amber and salt between the Lake District, Cornwall and Wales and the rest of the country used the Portway as one of their long distance routes in prehistoric times.

The close proximity of many of these barrows to the Portway suggests that they also acted as route markers along the line of the track. Others have suggested that they acted as boundary markers between different owners of land. This suggests that the trackway predates the barrows by some considerable time. For much of its length, the

Aerial view of the Long Mynd to the north west showing the Portway (the middle track)
Inset: Polished Neolithic stone axe found near the Portway, length 18 cm.

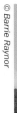

Shooting Butts disc barrow, so named because a grouse shooting hide was built on it in Victorian times when the hill was a grouse moor. The barrow is 2.3 m high and 21 m diameter. ^{14}C dating of the lowest level of charcoal in buried soil within the barrow gives it a date 1,690±45 BC.

Portway is the parish boundary between Church Stretton on the east and Ratlinghope, Wentnor and Myndtown on the west. The name derives from the Old English *porte* meaning town, mostly referring to market towns, i.e. 'the way to the market'.

Linear Earthworks

Three linear earthworks or cross-dykes at Devil's Mouth, Barrister's Plain and at High Park Cottage (at GRs 440943, 426928 and 444966 respectfully) are unusual archaeological features. They are well defined banks of earth and stone, up to a metre high in places, several hundred metres long and have a ditch on one or both sides. They are thought to be territorial boundary markers demarcating land allotment within communities and they may also have been used for controlling the movement of livestock between the plateau and the cultivated land and homesteads in the Stretton valley. They date from the late Bronze Age to early Iron Age period.

The Devil's Mouth on The Burway is the gap through which the road passes on the north side of Burway Hill. At this place, the effect of warm air from the valley meeting cold air from the plateau can create a localised dense mist. The name is said to originate from the tradition that the devil travelled in smoke and mist[2].

The Devil's Mouth linear earthwork is particularly impressive and is sited across a gap through which the old packhorse route from Church Stretton to the west side of the Long Mynd passed. The dyke is 140 m long and terminates where the precipitous slopes of Townbrook Valley (to the south) and Carding Mill Valley (to the north) render it unnecessary. It was a boundary marker and probably also used to control access along this old route, known today as The Burway. This gets its name from the Old English *burh* meaning fort because the road passed in sight of Bodbury Ring hill fort.

The Devil's Mouth linear earthwork (southern section), overlooks Townbrook Valley.

The Bodbury Ring hill fort with Caer Caradoc, a larger hill fort, in the background.

The Iron age (700 BC to AD 43)

Towards the end of the Bronze Age it is thought that the first hill forts appeared. These may have begun as settlements or livestock compounds but became well-defended sites and continued into the Iron Age. It is not known if these were permanent settlements or refuges but that on Caer Caradoc is thought to have been a permanent settlement as hut platforms can still be seen outlined within the fort. There are over fifty such forts in south Shropshire on most of the hilltops, the highest concentration in Britain.

Bodbury Ring is a hill fort occupying a strong defensive position on a steep sided promontory on the north side of Carding Mill Valley. It is situated opposite the larger hill fort of Caer Caradoc on the eastern side of the Stretton Valley. Only the local lord or chief, his family and retainers lived in the hill forts under normal conditions; the rest of the population lived elsewhere, although their dwellings are rarely found.

Artist's impression of Bodbury Ring hill fort as it might have originally looked. Caer Caradoc hill fort is in the background.

There is good evidence that members of the local Cornovii tribe in the late Bronze and Iron Ages were farming on the Long Mynd. Patterns of Celtic field systems at the south end of the Long Mynd overlooking the Onny Valley near Black Knoll have been discovered. The site covers 32 ha spanning 2,000 years of usage, the most impressive part being the late Iron Age/ Roman period field system complete with an interlocking system of track ways and an associated settlement. It is situated near a spring and there are sites of twelve houses or other buildings,

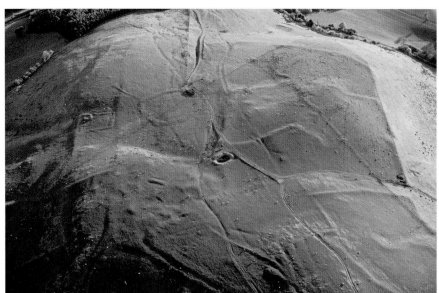

Black Knoll from the air, showing the outline of Celtic field systems and settlement. The white dots are sheep.

some with associated courtyards. Together, the fields and settlement provide dramatic evidence for arable farming on the Long Mynd over an extensive period. With the introduction of rabbits by the Normans, these hill slopes were also used for rabbit farming in the form of a 65 m diameter banked enclosure which was probably the rabbit warren. Another nearby enclosure is still called Warren House.

Another interesting Iron Age set of earthworks is the Stitt Hill Castle Ring on the north west edge of the Long Mynd near Ratlinghope. It was once thought to be a hill fort as the name suggests because of the cross-ridge dykes and rampart but it is now considered to be too weak to be used for defence against an aggressor. Instead, these earthworks were probably used to divide up pastureland and control movements of livestock. Throughout its long history, Castle Ring has also been used for agriculture. Within the Castle Ring enclosure it is possible to make out the tell-tale ridge and furrow corrugated markings indicative of medieval ploughing techniques.

The ancient monuments on the Long Mynd represent one of the richest and best preserved resources for understanding the prehistoric society of the West Midlands. There are over 80 recognised ancient monuments on the hill of which English Heritage has scheduled over 30 of them.

The Stitt Hill Cross-Dyke and Castle Ring showing the outline of the medieval ridge and furrow ploughing.

The Romans (AD 43 to c.410)

Evidence for settlement and land use in the Roman and early medieval period on the Long Mynd and in the Stretton valley is scarce although they were drawn to South Shropshire by the existence of minerals, especially lead, around the Stiperstones. The only archaeological evidence is the discovery of some Roman coins mainly of Emperor Constantine (early fourth century) found on Wildmoor. It is likely that the Long Mynd was grazed by sheep and cattle throughout this period from settlements located in the valleys.

Whilst the Romans made little impact on the Long Mynd itself, the military road that they built through the Stretton valley, Watling Street, which ran from Viroconium (Wroxeter) to Caerleon in South Wales, was an important highway; parts of it are still in existence. Although the road was not built for the local population, it would have had an impact on those living nearby. It is thought that cattle formed the economic base of Wroxeter, the fourth largest city in Roman Britain. It had a population of over 5,000 and acted as a market linking the highland and lowland regions of England to which the Long Mynd livestock may well have made a contribution.

The Anglo Saxons (7th to 11th centuries)

The next peoples to invade Britain were the Angles and Saxons who eventually reached this area by the seventh century. It is not certain to what extent the Celtic inhabitants were displaced but it was at best only partial. The Long Mynd lay in the Kingdom of Powys until about AD 630 and Welsh was spoken as far east as Shrewsbury and Bewdley up to the 18th century suggesting a Celtic rather than Anglo Saxon ancestry for much of the population. Conflict between the Celts and the invaders continued until the arrival of the Normans. The place names Walton and Walcot are derived from *walh*, a derogatory Anglo Saxon term for Celts.

However, with the arrival of the Anglo Saxons the countryside underwent major changes. The single fortified farms surrounded by fields which had become a feature of the Iron Age were superseded and new settlements began to appear in groups which grew into villages and hamlets surrounded by common fields. These new settlements typically had names ending in 'ton'. It is interesting that Minton and Myndtown have 'Mynd' as a root which suggests the name of the hill was in use in the eighth century and established at an early date.

The Normans

The Normans subjugated the local population with a Norman lord of the manor replacing a Saxon one. They formalised the feudal system whereby the lord protected the serfs and villeins who worked the land in return for their labour. The manor took a share of the annual harvest but the villeins were allowed to keep their own harvest from individually cultivated strips to which they had tenants rights. The serfs had fewer rights and worked directly for the lord.

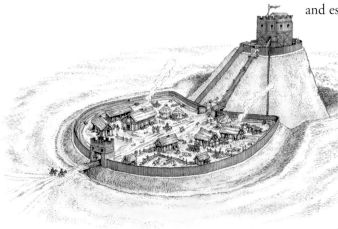

Artist's impression of a Norman motte and bailey castle.

© Barrie Raynor

The remains of the motte and bailey castle at Minton. Much of the motte remains but the wooden keep and bailey have long since been lost.

Some motte and bailey castles were built along the northern and eastern edges of the Long Mynd by Earl Roger de Montgomery, King William's cousin. He had been given the responsibility to defend this strategically important border region called the Middle Marches. The castle at Minton and another at All Stretton situated on what is now called Castle Hill were typical and comprised the motte, a circular conical mound of earth surmounted by a tall timber tower at its centre. Adjoining the motte were one or more baileys, enclosures defended by a palisaded bank and ditch to house the stores, stabling and accommodation of the garrison. They soon fell into disrepair and were abandoned by the thirteenth century leaving, in the case of Minton, just the earth mound. On Castle Hill, a most impressive site for a castle, there are no detectable remains.

The Manorial System and Parishes

By the time the Domesday Book was compiled in AD 1086, the manorial system was well established throughout most of England. A manor was the area of land that was held by feudal tenure by a landlord who was not necessarily noble but who was a tenant under the Crown (or another lord who held land directly from the Crown). Lords of the manor held their manor in return for military service and payments to the Crown.

From the ninth century onwards many manorial lords founded churches to serve their estates; the boundaries of these estates naturally developed as boundaries of church parishes. As landholdings were always in a state of transition, so parish boundaries were not always clear and disputes were common.

In cases where a lord had not built a church or where manors had been sub-divided, then some parishes may have included several manors. The only Domesday manor adjacent to the Long Mynd which recorded a church was that of Stretton-en-le-Dale (Church Stretton). The parishes of Wentnor and Smethcott did not appear until after the Domesday survey and took their names from the manor lying within them. Church Pulverbatch is an example of a parish containing several manors, namely Pulverbatch, Wrentnall, Wilderley and Cothercott, all of which have given their name to townships.

Much of the Long Mynd east of the Portway is in the parish of Church Stretton. Other parishes surrounding the Long Mynd are Myndtown, Wentnor and Ratlinghope to the west, and Church Pulverbatch, Smethcott, Woolstaston and Leebotwood to the north.

Long ago in areas where parish boundaries were not defined by some natural feature, marker stones or tumps (mounds of stones and earth) were built to define the boundary. A line of tumps marked the boundary on the western slope of the Long Mynd between the parishes of Wentnor and Ratlinghope. Some of these, albeit somewhat flattened, are still visible.

The old custom of 'beating the bounds' on Rogation Sunday was an annual survey carried out by parish officials to confirm the boundary of each parish and check that markers were still in existence.

Ancient stone on the Portway near Betchcott Hill marking the boundary of the manor of Cothercott. The stone once had a plaque saying
Township of Batchcott,
Manor of Cothercott,
T J Powys, Esq, 1791

The old drove road from the Portway to Minton.

Churchmoor

The Common Land

IN EARLY medieval times, much of the Long Mynd was part of the Royal Forest which stretched from Shrewsbury and Cressage to Craven Arms and called the Long Forest. Forest in this context meant land outside (that is, between) any manors within the forest area and was not necessarily woodland. Hunting in the forest for deer, wild boar, hare and wolf was reserved for the king and his friends. Forest law was enforced by foresters (stewards) and there were severe penalties for any transgression. Many areas withdrew from this jurisdiction by agreement and villagers then enjoyed common rights of grazing in the forest. Eventually these areas became subsumed into the adjacent manors but the ordinary villagers retained their common rights.

Despite the lords of the various manors owning different sectors of the Long Mynd, the ordinary peasants in the manors had a common right to allow their stock to graze upon waste or unproductive land but the number of animals permitted depended on how much manorial land they occupied in the valley. In addition they could hunt, gather natural resources such as wood, fruits, nuts, fungi, bracken and peat.

The common grazing rights were jealously guarded and passed down by the tenants through many generations and recorded in the court rolls (manorial records). Although the land was owned by the lord of the manor, the grazing rights belonged, and indeed still do, to those people who 'occupy land now or previously copyhold of the manor'; they were not available to all inhabitants of Church Stretton and other parishes adjacent to the Long Mynd.

It had become the habit over the centuries for many manorial lords to illegally fence off or enclose part of the common land on the Long Mynd which was crucial for the tenants' survival. Some time around 1610, riots had broken out in Church Stretton and neighbouring villages which were triggered by a threat of the loss of these commoners' rights.

Medieval shepherds each looked after a flock of about 240 sheep, with extra helpers to shear, wash and milk the ewes. Eventually there became a need to identify each ewe and so owners were obliged to mark or brand their stock or risk confiscation. Red sandstone was often used for making identification

Common land near the top of Townbrook Valley.

Sunrise.

marks on the sheep and bells were hung around their necks to enable the shepherds to keep track of them. The medieval earthworks on Nover's Hill may have been built as a stock enclosure to pen the flocks before they were brought down to the valley.

At that time, sheep were much more prone to disease than other stock and losses in bad years could be devastating. Supplementary feed was provided in the form of hay, peas, vetches, oats and bran. Tallow and oils were used to waterproof the sheep and tar pitch, verdigris and other ointments were used to treat cuts, sheep scab and foot rot.

The Medieval Wool Merchants

By the thirteenth and fourteenth centuries, Shropshire's wool merchants were amongst the wealthiest in the country and they traded large quantities of high quality wool with European cloth manufacturers. One of the leading Shropshire merchants was the Earl of Arundel who owned the Manor of Stretton-en-le-Dale which covered most

of the parish of Church Stretton and extended across the Long Mynd as far as the Portway to the west and to Minton Batch in the south. Beyond this boundary, other lords owned the land in the adjacent parishes.

In 1175, Henry II granted the monks of Haughmond Abbey the right to pasture their herd of horses on the Long Mynd. The Abbey also began to acquire many of the small manors on the north and west sides of the Long Mynd in the parishes of Leebotwood, Church Pulverbatch, Smethcott, Ratlinghope and Wentnor to form the combined manor of Boveria. Vast flocks of sheep belonging to the Abbey were driven onto the Long Mynd establishing it as a major source of wool and making the Shropshire wool merchants the richest in England. The monastic link was abruptly severed in the sixteenth century with the dissolution of the monasteries whereupon the manor was divided and sold. During this time, the Long Mynd provided the manorial lords with ideal land for grazing their large flocks of sheep at no additional cost and it provided a major source of income for the Abbey.

Markets

A WEEKLY market has been held in Church Stretton since 1214 and was the occasion for trading wool, livestock and produce. There were also markets and annual fairs at Bishop's Castle (since 1249), Clun (since 1204), Pulverbatch (since 1254) and Leebotwood (since 1320). A weekly livestock market still takes place in Bishop's Castle though the big autumn sheep sales ceased in Church Stretton about 1982.

Many of the tracks across the Long Mynd were used by local people with laden ponies to take produce to the nearest market. One long-distance traveller with goods for market was the huckster with his packhorse, the legacy from this era being track markers like the Packetstone (an exposed rock on the bridleway from Minton to Asterton) and the Huckster Stone (on the bridleway from Minton to Myndtown).

Trackways and the Welsh Drovers

It was the responsibility of parishes to maintain all roads within the parish irrespective of whether they were used just by parishioners or by travellers

using the main highways. The Portway was one of the roads that had the status of being part of the 'King's Highway on Longemunede' which entitled it to enjoy royal protection. In a manorial document dated 1278 it was referred to as the *Via Regalis.*

In the 18th century Welsh drovers who were herding hundreds of cattle to Shrewsbury markets were not prepared to pay the new tolls on the turnpike through the Stretton valley. To avoid this route, they once again used the old hill routes which linked up with the Portway. Overnight stops were at regular sites where there was an enclosure and accommodation. The *Pound Inn* at Leebotwood was one such stop and so got its name. The drovers used corgi dogs specially bred to work with cattle. These dogs were nimble and would snap at the heels of the cows, and being small with short legs, they avoided being kicked by the cows. In the 19th century the Portway was still being used by horses and wagons carrying agricultural produce to market; this continued until the opening of the Shrewsbury to Hereford railway in 1852.

© Oonagh O'Neill

Poorer market-goers had to walk to market. This woman uses her horse to transport produce from her smallholding on the other side of the Long Mynd to the market in Church Stretton. Contrast her rough working clothes with the group of ladies sporting the fashions of the day. (Burway Road, about 1900).

Another important old trackway on the Long Mynd was The Burway, an old packhorse route which ascends to the Portway from Church Stretton. It is a route probably used since prehistoric times because of the location of the Bronze Age cross-dyke at Devil's Mouth (see page 9). It is marked on Ogilby's road map of 1660 as part of the road from Bridgenorth, through Church Stretton to Welshpool. The old road survives as a wide trackway above the modern Burway Road.

Other ancient packhorse routes include that from All Stretton which followed the existing metalled lane as far as Jinlye from where it cuts across the plateau and through the High Park Cottage cross-dyke to the Portway. Another route went from Little Stretton up Small Batch and through the Barrister's Plain cross-dyke to the Portway at Pole Cottage. There was also another route from Minton to the Portway skirting Packetstone Hill.

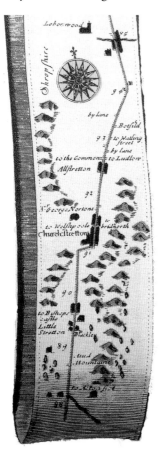

The old packhorse route up The Burway is now a wide path. The new paved road with a gentler gradient is lower down to the left.

Part of Ogilby's road map of 1660 showing the road at Church Stretton which goes to Welshpool over the Long Mynd via The Burway and the road eastwards to Bridgnorth.

One of several drover's routes on the west side of the Long Mynd lined with ancient beeches.

© Barrie Raynor

© Barrie Raynor

Enclosure of Land

IN THE LATE 18th century many owners of land tried to enclose what were the traditional open fields and commons, the object being to improve the land and increase their revenues. Attempts at enclosing some of the common land on the Long Mynd were made in 1788 following the Parliamentary Act 'for enclosing certain commons and waste lands in the manor of Stretton' but due to the commoners' strongly held rights and partly because of the increasing importance and popularity of grouse shooting, the open heath land remained unenclosed.

The Napoleonic Wars (1793–1815) caused an increased domestic demand for grain, as well as increases in prices and rents, to unprecedented levels. To help alleviate this, marginal land previously under pasture was brought into cultivation wherever possible. Some of the land on the Long Mynd, used now by the golf course, is relatively flat and was used to grow grain during this period but the cultivation of this area was abandoned after about four years because the soil became so poor. The ploughed ridge and furrow strips (narrow rig) can still be seen now that the area has reverted to pasture.

The Long Mynd has always been highly prized by the lords of the manor and their sporting tenants. The combination of many people having common rights and the good shooting has resulted in such a large area of open common land remaining an unfenced and open area to this day.

In the 1870s during another period of poverty amongst the farming community, there was little grazing which resulted in some natural regrowth of trees as evidenced by the numerous hawthorns in many of the valleys all dating from that period.

Commoners' Rights

The Church Stretton Commoners' Association was formed in 1868 with the aim of enforcing long-standing

© Robin Jukes-Hughes

Ploughed ridge and furrow strips on the golf course below Bodbury Ring have now reverted to pasture.

rules such as not leaving animals on the hill in winter and to deal with trespassing and encroachments. One person in 1566 had been fined for unlawfully wintering sheep and another for overburdening the common, both 'to the injury of all the township'.

Cattle and goats had been banned from the hill at some stage and were subject to a formal ban in 1908. Names such as Cow Ridge, Calf Ridge, Yearlet and Bullocksmoor which have existed for centuries provide evidence that cattle were once grazed on the hill; it is believed that 19th century lords of the manor banned them because they were damaging the shooting butts. As a result of this ban the bracken spread.

By 1913, the Commoners' Association had members from Ratlinghope and within a few years had agreed to extend their powers over those portions of the Long Mynd that lay within the Ratlinghope and Wentnor estates of the Scott family which were up for sale. At the time of this sale, the occupiers of three of the farms each had rights of turnout for 100 sheep and 10 ponies, twenty other smaller holdings had smaller rights, in all amounting to 1,035 sheep and 102 ponies. Little wonder Church Stretton had also been in dispute with Ratlinghope two hundred years earlier when one tenant had 900 sheep on the Long Mynd!

In 1965, under the Commons Registrations Act, 106 commoners claimed their right (probably exaggerated) to graze 24,299 sheep, 148 cattle and 1,146 ponies on the Long Mynd, a level of grazing which would clearly be unsustainable though not all of these people exercised that right. By 1992, there were only 18 commoners with 13,609 sheep actually grazing on the Long Mynd that year. Such stocking levels, a result of European Union subsidy payments to hill farmers, were 5½ times the level that the common could sustain and was destroying the historic vegetation that had resulted from centuries of manorial management.

Fortunately, in 2000 under the Environmentally Sensitive Areas (ESA) scheme, an agreement was reached with the active graziers to limit the number of ewes to 3,341 in the summer and 1,670 in the winter. Those farmers who were not using their right voluntarily gave up that right. These figures approximate to the sort of sheep numbers on the Long Mynd during the twentieth century up to 1965.

The common is now used exclusively for sheep together with about 30 ponies, far fewer than there once were. As a result of these measures, the grass, heather and bilberry cover has made a remarkable recovery. It should be added that the commoner's rights never included mineral nor sporting rights.

In 1965, Minton Hill and the manor of Stretton-en-le-Dale were bought by the National Trust by a public appeal and, as the current owner of the Long Mynd, the National Trust is the lord of the manor. In subsequent years, it bought land in The Batch (1978), Carding Mill Valley and Bodbury Hill (1979), the Wern (1993), Handless Bank (1998) and other small parcels of land.

Unfortunately, in 2001, foot and mouth disease struck the northern part of the Long Mynd and it was without stock for many months.

Sheep with winter feed.

Long Mynd Habitats

ALL THE factors, both natural and man made, described in the preceding pages have had an effect on what the Long Mynd looks like and the habitats that it sustains today. There are several different semi-natural habitats within the boundary of the Long Mynd each supporting a different type of wildlife. Rocky outcrops such as Junction Rock support a characteristic community of lichens and mosses whilst other habitats are dependent on the nature of the soil layer. The soils on the plateau are shallow and acidic because of the chemical composition of the underlying rock. They are deficient in nitrates, phosphates and lime and provide a low level of fertility. The clearing of the broad-leafed woodland trees initiated podzolisation, the formation of a hard ferrous or alumina-rich hard pan under blanket peat which affects all the habitats.

Upland Heath

The plateau area is described as dry heath because it is largely well-drained except in the small depressions and the areas around the natural springs. By contrast, moorland is defined as having deep peat often up to several metres deep and usually associated with cooler, damper climates. The heath on the Long Mynd is dominated by heather (ling, *Calluna vulgaris)* and bilberry. The proportion of heather declines towards the edges of the plateau giving way to bilberry. This is a result of heavy grazing by sheep in the past because the bilberry is more resilient to grazing. Provided that the density of sheep can be kept low, there is evidence for recovery of heather amongst the bilberry.

Valley Sides

The north and south facing slopes of those valleys draining eastwards are subtly different, a difference which arises from the after-effects of the last ice age. In the centuries during which the ice sheets were melting, the ground was still frozen with ice filling the cracks in the rock and penetrating cleavage planes. On warmer days there would be some melting at the surface and re-freezing at night. As water freezes it expands by 9%, the force of which is enough to crack open rock and cleave the stratified layers which make up the Long Mynd rock. The repeated freezing and thawing breaks the rock into progressively smaller pieces.

South facing slopes get more sun each day than north facing slopes and so more of the trapped ice will melt. With a continuous cycle of freezing and thawing there will be progressive fracturing of the rock. The result is loose rock which may fall and create scree slopes. These warmer south facing slopes are better drained than those which face north. As a result, they typically have more gorse and distinctive grassland communities have developed there.

The upper slopes, particularly those facing north have heather or bilberry or short grass with abundant lichens, whilst those lower down are mainly covered with grass and bracken. Bracken is particularly noticeable in the autumn when it turns a rich brown as it dies back for the winter.

Overall, the valleys support a fairly rich and diverse flora and fauna because of the range of habitats existing. There is often a scattering of old hawthorn trees and an abundance of small spring annuals and plants such as harebell and wild thyme.

© NT Shropshire Hills

This view of Carding Mill Valley looking east shows the difference in vegetation cover between the well-drained south-facing slope (left) and the north-facing slope (right) covered in heather and bilberry.

Upland Acid Grassland

The mixture of short and medium grass and scattered tussocks of siliceous mat grass provides an ideal habitat for wildlife. The mat grass provides shelter in winter for insects and nest sites for skylarks.

Most of the upland acid grassland and bracken is associated with the steep valley sides. On these slopes, the proportion of bilberry relative to bracken increases with altitude, then grades into grass-heath and then heath proper. These boundaries are indistinct but the trends are apparent as one walks up a valley to the plateau.

The upland grassland typically consists of a mixture of wavy hair-grass, sheep's fescue and common bent, with tussocks of mat grass, a tough grass which sheep avoid eating if at all possible. This tussocky grass is a better habitat for wildlife than the short uniform sward which is closely grazed by the sheep and has a tight springy structure. Flowers associated with the grasses include heath bedstraw, sheep's sorrel tormentil, heath speedwell and mountain pansy.

Much of the grassland is the result of past intensive grazing by sheep which has suppressed the growth of dwarf shrubs and trees. With the reduction in sheep numbers, much of the former grassland is beginning to revert back to grass-heath and heath.

Rock Outcrops and Associated Open Grassland

Some of the richest and most interesting vegetation on the Long Mynd is associated with the numerous small outcrops of rock and areas of bare, loose scree. These occur on the steep valley slopes and on the tops of ridges which separate the valleys. They support a flower-rich acidic grassland community very different from the grass-dominated upper slopes and include thyme, harebell, mouse-ear hawkweed and lady's bedstraw. Bedstraws get their name because they were once put into straw mattresses to add fragrance.

Rocky outcrops also host an interesting selection of mosses, lichens and spring arrivals such as shepherd's cress. bird's-foot trefoil and parsley piert.

Rust-red swathes of sheep's sorrel cover upland grassland in June.

Other typical upland grassland flowers:

Above: heath bedstraw, and mountain pansy,

Below: tormentil and heath speedwell.

© Lis Burke

© Natureblogger.com

© Anne Burgess

© David Baird

© Anne Burgess

© Gary Rogers

© Andrew Curtis

Flowers associated with rock outcrops and dry hillsides.

Above: thyme, Right: wall pennywort (named because the size of the leaves is that of the old penny coin).

Below: mouse-ear hawkweed, bird's-foot trefoil, produmbent pearlwort.

Bottom: harebell, lady's bedstraw.

Heather and its Management

Heather dominates the extensive tract of heath land which covers the main part of the Long Mynd plateau and is in full bloom in August and September. The term heather strictly refers to members of the genus *Calluna* but it is also used as a general term for heaths such as cross-leaved heath, found only in wet places, and bell heather which is very rare on the plateau. The most abundant is ling which is distinguished from these other heathers by having tiny stalkless scale-like leaves which hug the shoots and by having small pink-purple sepals which line the shoot tips.

Some insects, grouse and many small mammals depend on ling for food and cover. On the Long Mynd, grouse management involves cutting or burning areas so that the new shoots provide food for grouse. This is being done between areas of older heather which are left to provide quickly accessible cover for the grouse. Grouse do not like to be further than 15 m from cover when feeding and so cutting or burning is carried out in irregularly-shaped strips which are less than 30 m wide; this explains the mosaic of different aged plants visible on the plateau.

The National Trust aims to actively manage 60% of the heather over a 15–18 year cycle thus providing heather with a range of different ages. The remaining 40% is left as old growth in order to encourage grouse because they like old heather to nest amongst. In addition, leaving some old heather allows slow growing species such as lichens to provide nesting sites for smaller birds as well as a habitat for amphibians, small mammals, reptiles and invertebrates, all of which could be lost by burning. Fortunately there is now clear evidence that this management regime has resulted in an increase in grouse numbers.

Heather cutting.

Heather burning.

Natural regeneration of heather and other plants after the trees at Handless had been cut down.

Old heather more than 20 years old does not recover after cutting because it is too woody. New heather grows from seed which is lying dormant in the soil, albeit slowly. In the conifer plantation at Handless and at the Wern, the conifers have been felled and heather seedlings have, after five years, burst through the dense carpet of pine needles and the area is now returning to heath land naturally.

Ling has been much used by humans over the years for herbal remedies, brooms, thatching, ropes, bedding, dyeing leather (yellow) and making heather ale. One of the best known products in recent years is heather honey and in many parts of Britain beehives are moved onto heather moorland at flowering time. Heather honey can command twice the price of other British honeys.

Ling's genus name, *Calluna*, is derived from the Greek word *kallunein* meaning to cleanse. This probably refers to its use in brooms. The word ling comes from the Norse *lyng* meaning light (in weight). This came about because heather turf was much lighter than grass turf when cut for fuel. Heather is seen as iconic of Scotland where the plant grows widely and where poems like *Bonnie Auld Scotland* speak of 'fragrant hills of purple heather'.

Prior to the acquisition of much of the Long Mynd by the National Trust, it was a shooting estate. The heather moor was managed to preserve and provide for the needs of grouse. Moorland is therefore not a habitat threatened by human activity but rather one that exists because of it.

Heather Beetle Control

Mild, wet winters and summers can produce problems with heather beetle and the damage that this causes to heather is a periodic worry. This beetle hibernates throughout the winter below the surface and emerges in spring. It feeds on heather and lays eggs on damp ground, particularly sphagnum moss, and then dies. By late May the eggs hatch into grubs. These then invade the heather plants eating young shoots and damaging stems with the result that by July the heather turns an orange-red colour before dying and going completely grey by the following spring. Seedlings and old heather are especially vulnerable to attack, leaving only young,

Heather beetle.

Bilberry (whinberry).

vigorously growing heather capable of surviving. By early August the grubs start to drop off the heather and bury into the litter to pupate into the adult beetle.

Notwithstanding the damage that can be done by heather beetle, nature does have its own mechanism for keeping it in check. There is a small wasp that lays up to 15 eggs in young heather beetle grubs. These then hatch into parasitic larvae and infest the grubs. They have the effect of making the grubs leave the heather prematurely therefore doing less damage. Adult wasps emerge from the grubs in the following spring and attack the next generation of heather beetle grubs as they climb out of the litter. It is perhaps for this reason that heather beetle attacks are cyclical in nature.

Bilberry

Along with ling, bilberry likes acid moors and woods and is one of the most common plants on the Long Mynd. Although these two plants look quite different, they are both members of the same plant family, *Ericaceae*. Bilberry is readily identified by the bright apple-green colour of its foliage and by its photosynthetic stems which are of a similar colour and persist leafless through the winter. The tiny urn-shaped flowers are only about 6 mm long and pink in colour. In July and August, the ovaries of the flowers ripen into black berries with a violet bloom which can be picked patiently one by one or with a special comb and scoop.

Bilberries have a range of alternative regional names such as whortleberry, blaeberry, blackheart, blackwort and huckleberry. Locally, they are called wimberry or whinberry, a term used in Wales, Shropshire and Lancashire. The ancient Britons used the juice to stain their faces and was used later as a blue dye for linen and paper. On the Long Mynd, bilberries were a useful crop and picking them provided a lot of employment for local people in the nineteenth and early twentieth century. Large quantities were sold to the Lancashire cotton factories for fabric dyeing. Locally they were used for dyeing the rough woollen blankets once made in Carding Mill Valley.

Bilberry fungal plant disease

A worrying fungal infection on bilberry plants causes the roots to rot and the plant to wilt and have discoloured foliage and stems. It is a non-native disease found mainly in trees in the United States and continental Europe. It was first recorded in Britain in 2005 affecting a small number of trees, mainly larch, and on bilberry plants on Cannock Chase in Staffordshire but has now spread to the Long Mynd. At present there is no treatment for the disease and the only way to eradicate it is to completely kill all affected bilberry plants to prevent the disease spreading.

Research is being carried out to determine the most effective method of control, probably herbicide or fungicide, but quickly limiting the spread of the disease is paramount. Fortunately the disease is harmless to humans, wildlife and livestock even when eaten, although all these groups can spread the infection through contact.

Bracken Control on the Long Mynd

Bracken was formerly much scarcer than at present and once called brake fern. Sometime around the time of the industrial revolution it jumped from a woodland-edge species to an open-hill species and is now the largest organism on earth and found everywhere except Antarctica.

Over half the Long Mynd is covered by bracken. It is an invasive fern which, if left to spread unchecked, much of the Long Mynd would soon become covered by it. It thrives because it is not eaten by any of the animals; sheep trampling does not damage it in the way that cattle trampling would and the ponies are too few to have a significant effect. Also, the farmers no longer cut bracken for use as bedding for livestock. Bracken is a perennial and spreads because of its underground rhizomes or spreading root system which covers a huge area; it is, however, a valuable carbon store. Bracken also harbours high levels of ticks which bite and may transmit Lyme disease to humans. This disease is showing a rapid increase in Britain but as yet it is not a problem on the Long Mynd.

Cutting bracken using a double-chop harvester.

© Nick Robinson

Bracken control is therefore a major concern of the National Trust. Where bracken grows amongst acid grassland, for example on the northern and eastern sides of the hill, the bracken is mown on a regular basis. This does not eliminate the plant but reduces its vigour and prevents further encroachment. On the Long Mynd, about 30 ha of bracken is harvested annually in late July using a double-chop harvester after birds have finished nesting.

The cut bracken is taken to a nearby farm for composting where the conditions are carefully monitored so that the decaying bracken reaches a temperature of 60 °C for 3 weeks and 30 °C for 9 weeks. This is essential to make sure that any traces of the naturally occurring carcinogen ptaquiloside, which concentrates in the young shoots (fiddleheads or croziers) and may remain in the mature bracken, are broken down. It is these young shoots which are particularly poisonous to animals who may eat them or are tempted to if there is nothing else to eat. The compost produced is ready for sale in the August of the following year and sold under the name of 'Green Frond: the environmental answer to bracken control'. The aim is to make a commercial product out of a problem species in an environmentally friendly way.

By trying to control bracken on top of the hill, the National Trust is hoping to push it outwards and down the valley sides. This allows regeneration of grass and heather on the top and is already proving successful on Plush Hill.

Nevertheless, bracken provides an important habitat for a few rare species, especially fritillary butterflies and whinchats. Whinchats are summer visitors which nest in leaf litter below thick bracken. Such conditions occur in many places on the Long Mynd and 120 pairs of these birds nest here. This makes the area a nationally important upland site with the largest concentration of whinchats in this part of England.

Originally bracken was gathered for cattle bedding, protecting pottery during transportation, mulching potato beds, for fuel, and the ashes used in soap making and glass manufacture.
The Bracken Gathers, *by Kate Greenaway*

© Barrie Raynor

© Forest & Kim Starr

Common European gorse.

Gorse

In summer and autumn many of the valley hillsides are bright with the yellow almond-scented flowers of the prickly western gorse. Much of it is very old and stands up to 1.5 m high. Unfortunately where there are large swathes of gorse there is almost complete loss of grass and lichens beneath it. Where it grows in dense patches it can be a fire hazard because it burns very easily. The National Trust has a programme of periodically burning older bushes to make a fire break and allow regeneration of the stems from where new growth starts as well as opening up a habitat for rare grassland species. There is also a small amount of common European gorse which flowers mainly in the winter and spring. Overall, there is always gorse in bloom somewhere in the valley and this gives rise to the old country proverb

When gorse is out of blossom, kissing's out of fashion.

Gorse is unusual in having prickles instead of leaves but despite the prickly nature of the shrub, sheep and horses sometimes eat it with the result that many of the bushes have become rounded. With the reduction in sheep numbers since 2000, sheep have less need to eat it except as a last resort.

Gorse is a member of the pea family and when dry the brittle pea-like pods explode in the sun or by fire throwing out seeds for several feet. Like other members of the pea family, gorse is capable of fixing atmospheric nitrogen and so is a useful plant. Gorse goes by other names such as whin, furse and furze though the name itself is from the Old English *gorst* meaning waste referring to the shrub's natural habitat of moorland and common.

In the past, bundles of gorse branches (faggots) were used in baking ovens because they burnt very hot and they were also used to sweep chimneys. The ashes of gorse are rich in alkali and were used to make a rudimentary soap. There is much folklore about gorse based on its supposed ability to drive out witches and protection from curses.

Gorse is highly inflammable and a serious fire risk. It has to be cleared around property and fire-breaks made. These photos show controlled gorse burning on the steep side of Carding Mill Valley.

Trees

OVER MANY centuries, farmers have felled trees on the Long Mynd in order to provide building material, fuel and more pasture for their flocks of sheep. This accounts for the absence of trees on the plateau and relatively few in the valleys. There are scattered gnarled old hawthorn trees in most valleys as well as small clusters of mature common oak, sessile oak, Scots pine, ash and rowan. These are the remains of the original woodland cover of the Long Mynd. Patches of wood sorrel on the valley sides is further proof that there was once woodland on the Long Mynd.

Most of valleys have many hawthorn trees still standing which mostly date from the 1870s. This decade was a period of poverty and there were few animals on the Long Mynd which allowed tree seedlings to get established. There are also good stands of deciduous trees below Ashlet, at the Wern, in The Batch, Rectory Wood and on the hillside from All Stretton through to Little Stretton. These are all areas, however, which have traditionally been enclosed and not accessed by animals.

Now that the sheep numbers have been dramatically reduced in recent years, there is a significant regeneration of heather and bilberry together with the growth of new tree saplings. In fact, large numbers of young rowan trees are appearing on the west side of the Long Mynd in stands of tall dense heather and bracken where sheep cannot penetrate to graze. To increase the number of hawthorn trees which are such an important habitat, the National Trust has a programme of planting native tree species to supplement the existing sparse covering of trees.

In 2009, 27 kg of hawthorn berries were gathered and sent to Forestart, a specialist seed nursery, so that in a few years time saplings can be planted to replace the old and wizened hawthorn trees on the valley sides. A large stock of heather seed has also been collected and is used to re-seed areas where heather has been lost.

The Forestry Commission larch plantation at Handless Bank (near Asterton) was bought by the

© Robin Jukes-Hughes

Only a few trees remain in Ashes Hollow.

National Trust in 1998. The land has been cleared of conifers and natural regeneration of bilberry, heather and wavy hair-grass has taken place surprisingly quickly. The decaying tree stumps provide a habitat for longhorn beetles, ants, solitary bees and wasps.

The Wern, bought in 1993 is an enclosed wooded area of conifer plantation and mature deciduous trees. The conifers have been clear-felled together with a small plantation of poplars and the area has been left to regenerate naturally although there has been some planting of saplings.

It is interesting that as a result of the general warming of the climate in recent decades there has been a steady creep northwards of mistletoe. One of the hawthorn trees in Carding Mill Valley now has a large bunch growing on it.

Right: Mistletoe on an old hawthorn, Carding Mill Valley.

Below: Rectory Wood. A well-managed wood has a mixture of old and young trees. Fallen trees and branches are left to rot to recycle minerals and to provide a habitat for many invertebrates.

© Barrie Raynor

© Chris Stratton

Wet Areas: Springs, Mires, Flushes and Pools

THE LONG MYND contains several major streams. The largest on the eastern side, from north to south, are in The Batch and Jonathan's Hollow. Carding Mill Valley. Townbrook Valley, Ashes Hollow, Callow Hollow and Minton Batch. These all arise from springs near the western edge of the plateau and flow eastwards through steep-sided valleys. Most contain side valleys which are fed by numerous smaller streams and flushes which originate from spring heads high up on the valley slopes. On the western side, the principal streams are Darnford Brook and Bilbatch Brook.

Many of the springs follow lines of particular strata at the surface. Rainwater has, over the years, penetrated through the bedding planes of the underlying rock and, under the pressure of the weight of rock above it, been forced upwards and has escaped through cracks to reach the surface as springs. There are dozens of these springs on the Long Mynd and each is the source of flushes, mires, pools and eventually the main streams in each valley. One spring on the hill which bubbles constantly is called Boiling Well. This was where the gypsies used to camp when they were picking bilberries. It is difficult to find this spring today because of the marsh plants around it but it is the source of the stream in Ashes Hollow.

Flushes and Mires

The plateau is described as dry heath and huge areas on the plateau fit that description and is readily recognised by the abundant heather and bilberry present. There are, however, important areas of wetland. Mires (boggy areas) are fed by rain water or springs and are formed in hollows where there is impeded drainage because of the underlying rock. Here the water table is at or above ground level for most of the year.

Sphagnum mosses greatly influence the appearance and ecology of mires. These plants are intolerant of dry conditions and their stems and leaves contain

© Kate Johnson

Wildmoor Pool. Here, large stands of bottle sedge, characterised by having triangular stems, cover the pond.

networks of large, hollow cells which draw up water and retain it around the growing shoot-tips. These cells confer a sponge-like character which is very obvious if the saturated moss is squeezed. An abundance of sphagnum moss therefore accentuates soil waterlogging, creating oxygen-starved conditions which stifle the soil ecosystem. This in turn inhibits the breakdown of plant remains which gradually accumulate to form peat.

Flushes occur where there is water movement over or through the peaty surface. As the water trickles down the valley sides, nutrients that have leached from the soil becomes concentrated in drainage lines called flushes. Flushes are immediately recognised by the vertical line of rushes. They are mostly acidic and characterised by soft rush, bog mosses, and small sedges on the sides.

Marshy areas near streams and flushes are ecologically the richest and most diverse parts of the hill and contain

Right: One of many flushes in Townbrook Valley characterised by the rich vegetation, particularly rushes, in contrast with the adjacent dry heather and bracken.

Below: Common cotton grass is found in most boggy areas on the Long Mynd. It is not a grass but a member of the sedge family.

© Barrie Raynor

© Richard Burkmar

© Chris Stratton

Boggy areas (mires) are characterised by soft rush and many aquatic plants.

many small but interesting plants. For example butterwort and sundew are two insectivorous plants that need to catch small insects to help feed themselves because the soil and water in which they grow is not rich enough. They can trap insects on their sticky leaves and as the insect decays it will nourish the plant through its leaf.

Pools

Large stretches of open water are scarce on the Long Mynd and most of the pools are artificial, some made long ago to provide water for livestock on the common land but many were created to provide extinguishing water for heathland fires should incendiary bombs be dropped to guide German bombers during the Second World War. There are over 65 pools on the plateau, most of them are very small and well hidden. There is a group of pools behind the Pole Cottage enclosure originally excavated by the Earl of Powys around

© Pete Johnson

Dicranum moss.

Wetland and pond plants

Top left: The carnivorous common sundew in flower. It is found in several wet areas on the Long Mynd and is the county flower of Shropshire.

Top right: Soft rush in flower. This is the most common rush on the Long Mynd. Its pith, when soaked in mutton fat, was traditionally used as candles.

Bottom left: Round-leaf water-crowfoot.

Bottom right: Bogbean, so named from the roughly broad-bean-like shape of the leaves which were once used to treat rheumatism.

A typical shallow pond with bog pondweed and surrounded by rushes and mosses.

1900 as decoy ponds for wildfowling but the largest and most important is Wildmoor Pool which was created about 1850. It has been artificially dammed by the road to Upper Darnford above Colliersford Gutter.

All the ponds and pools support a wide range of flora and fauna. The pond edges merge into the surrounding flush vegetation. Typical aquatic plants include common spike-rush, soft rush, bottle sedge, water horsetail, bog pondweed, bogbean, round-leafed water crowfoot, water mint and water-cress and alternate water-milfoil which is scarce in Shropshire.

The ponds support a wide range of invertebrates such as water beetles, bugs, weevils and hoverflies, as well as dragonflies and palmate newts. A few pools on Wildmoor contain great-crested newts.

Pond life. Left: female black-tailed skimmer dragonfly.
Middle: a female great diving beetle. These beetles are huge, over 2 cm long and fiercely carnivorous being capable of eating baby frogs, newts and small fish.
Right: pond skaters can row themselves across the surface of water at high speed. Tiny claws on their feet spread out which gives them a larger area so that they do not penetrate the surface of the water.

© Scott Wilson

Butterwort is a carnivorous plant that has sticky tongue-shaped leaves which catch insects. It is one of the few plants to contain fat and was once used to curdle milk into butter. Abundant in Townbrook Valley.

© Silversyrpher

© Ferran Turmo Gort

Left: Backswimmers, often called water boatmen, swim on their backs. They have long back legs which they use as oars and are particularly fierce bugs which prey on tadpoles, small fish and insects.

Right: Whirligig beetles feed on small insects that fall into the water. They are much smaller and spin round and round on the surface of the water at a vast rate and sometimes dive down in spirals. Hilaire Belloc wrote:

But if he ever stopped to think
Of how he did it, he would sink.

Streams

The streams that flow in the valleys have a bed of bare rock covered by gravel, stones and small rocks. The water is well oxygenated, cool and fast flowing and is the ideal habitat for a host of nymphs, larvae and shrimps that bury themselves in the gravel and under the stones.

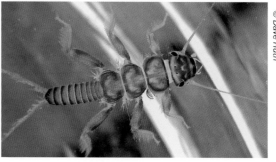

Brown trout are regular inhabitants of the streams and larger pools, mill ponds and reservoirs where they stay almost motionless, head upstream waiting for unsuspecting insects to be carried down to them. The bullhead, or miller's thumb, is much smaller and grows to no more than 15 cm long. The name alludes to its resemblance to the rough, swollen and gnarled appearance of a miller's thumb caused by his constant testing of the coarseness of his flour. Bullheads typically hide under flat stones and are well camouflaged against the gravel bottom of the streams, emerging to feed at dusk.

On the east side of the Long Mynd, Ash Brook (in Carding Mill Valley) and those streams to the north flow into the Cound Brook which drains into the Severn at Cound. Town Brook and those streams to the south flow into the Quinney Brook which drains into the Onny, then the Teme and eventually into the Severn at Worcester. On the west side all the streams drain south into the East Onny, a tributary of the Onny.

Top: Stonefly and its nymph (beneath). When they fly, they exhibit a characteristic lack of skill, travelling mostly in a straight line until they land or collide with something. They are often found sitting on stones near streams.

Left: Mayfly. The presence of both stonefly and mayfly is a sign of good clean-flowing water.

Below: Two of the species of fish in the Long Mynd streams are bullhead (left) and brown trout (right). Perch and roach are also found in the Town Brook reservoir.

© Mike Pennington

© NT Shropshire Hills

Flowers in wet areas

Far left: marsh marigold.

Left: teasel.

Above: bog pimpernel.

Below: lady's smock or cuckoo flower.

© Tom Joliffe

Bog asphodel. The old name for this plant is 'bonebreaker' because cattle feeding on the nutrient-poor places where it grows tended to develop bone deficiency diseases. In the 17th century women gathered it from the moors to use as a hair dye.

Woodland

© NT Shropshire Hills

Tree cover is very limited on the Long Mynd but is actually more significant than it might seem at first glance. There are, for example, over 1,200 hawthorn trees in Callow Hollow alone and there are many hawthorns and rowans in the other valleys.

Historic high grazing levels have had a severe impact on tree and shrub regeneration. The present tree age distribution suggests that this has been the situation for decades and few young hawthorn trees can be found, their tender shoots getting eaten by sheep. However, large numbers of young rowan trees are now appearing in stands of tall dense heather and bracken where sheep cannot penetrate to graze.

The former Forestry Commission larch plantation at Handless Bank on the western edge of the Long Mynd has been clear-felled after it was bought by the National Trust in 1998. Natural regeneration of heather, bilberry and some holly and rowan has, after five years, burst through the dense carpet of pine needles and has encouraged a return of many insects. The rotting tree stumps have also provided a valuable habitat for a range of beetles, bees and wasps.

Hopes Wood.

© Pete Johnson

The Wern, near Minton, was a mixed deciduous and conifer wood which was bought by the National Trust in 1993. The conifers and poplars have since been felled leaving the broad-leafed woodland and the understorey to develop naturally.

Most of the valleys, especially The Batch, are well wooded in their lower reaches as is most of the eastern side of the Long Mynd.

Fungi on this fallen oak help to recycle the minerals and other nutrients trapped in the tree.

© Chris Stratton

© Peter Carty

Typical woodland flora

Above: primroses in typical wood understory.

Left: musk mallow.

Below: garlic in Hopes Wood.

© NT Shropshire Hills

The Medieval Wood

In the Middle Ages, the woods around the edge of the Long Mynd would have been populated by woodcutters and domestic livestock. To our medieval forebears wood was a vital necessity of life second only to food. Wood was the raw material from which houses, carts, tool handles, domestic utensils, furniture, fencing and numerous other artefacts were made. Woodlands also provided a source of fuel for cooking and heating and because they were so important, most were legally protected and harsh punishments were handed down to the hapless individuals who cut trees without permission, stole wood and timber or allowed unauthorised animals to graze in woodlands.

The medieval economy ran on wood and a plentiful supply of wood was essential to sustain it. This was achieved by coppicing the trees, an ancient practice that can be traced back to the Neolithic period, some 5,000 years ago. Most of our native broad-leaved tree species have the capacity to grow new stems from cut stumps. Coppicing exploited this natural property as trees were periodically cut down to a stump (stool) and then left for a period of years to regrow. From the 15th until the late 19th century, coppicing was carried out to provide a continuous and sustainable supply of wood. Small trees (underwood) were cut on a short rotation of between 8 and 25 years to provide wood for fuel and raw materials. A number of trees were left uncut during the coppice cycle and allowed to grow to maturity to become constructional timber. Coppicing also provided the raw materials for charcoal-making and oak bark was used by the tanneries.

Coppiced woods are recognised by the old coppice stools which have grown into multi-stemmed trees like the hazel coppice illustrated below. Coppicing rejuvenated woods and lets light into the woodland to create the conditions which favoured the wild plants and the insects and birds that depend upon them.

Remnants of coppiced woods can be seen in The Batch at All Stretton as witnessed by their names Synalds Coppice, Open Coppice and Park Coppice.

Rectory Wood

Rectory Wood is part of a historic park formerly in the glebe of the Rector of Church Stretton. The well-preserved wood comprises woodland walks, a stream, an artificial pool and sites of buildings which include a pumping house and an ice house.

The Rector from 1749 to 1807, Professor John Mainwaring, had amongst his many friends Lancelot (Capability) Brown who visited him at the Rectory in 1775. Soon afterwards Mainwaring began to improve the glebe including Rectory Wood and it seems probable that at least informal guidance was provided by Brown. It is not certain which improvements are of that period and which were the responsibility of later 19th century Rectors. It seems likely, however, that it was in the earlier period that the Town Brook which ran

close to the northern boundary of the wood was dammed and a pool formed. It was probably also then that formal walks were laid out around the steeply sloping wooded hills, from which views out to the hills on the east side of Church Stretton could be enjoyed.

Rectory Wood was entered from the west side of the Rectory grounds via an elaborate stone gateway with a Gothic arch which is no longer in existence. A rockery surrounding a veteran sweet chestnut tree probably forms part of the entry complex. From there the path leads to the pool which is dark and still and shaded by yew trees. A stone weir controls the water height. On the north side of the pool is a ruined stone and brick building with Gothic windows which was built in the early 1760s as a folly or hermitage and is

© Barrie Raynor

The pond in Rectory Wood is surrounded by seven yew trees and once provided ice for the nearby icehouse for the Rectory.

shown on a 1767 plan. In 1865, it was converted to a pumping house which supplied Church Stretton with water when the reservoir higher up Townbrook Valley was built and continued in use until its replacement by that in New Pool Hollow in 1902.

The wood planted by Mainwaring was felled by a subsequent Rector, Rev'd Robert Norgrave Pemberton in the 1820s or 1830s and the trees were replaced by trees for timber, many of which still survive.

Both Rectory Wood and the adjoining Rectory Field are now owned by the Shropshire Council and are managed as public open spaces.

Below: Bluebells in Rectory Wood. These bluebells are the so-called English bluebell which has all its bell-like flowers drooping to one side of the stem. The invasive Spanish bluebell, not a naturalised British plant, is much stouter and erect and its flowers emerge from all sides of the stem.

Sheep and Ponies

THE LONG MYND would lose much of its character and appeal were it not for the sheep and ponies that graze and roam the valleys and plateau.

The sole agricultural use now of the Long Mynd is sheep farming. All of the open hill is common grazing land, which means that although the National Trust is the owner of about half of it, it does not own the grazing rights. Instead, these are held by the commoners who, in most cases, are now owners of agricultural land in the parishes surrounding the Long Mynd.

As a consequence of over-stocking until recent years, the heathland vegetation was in decline, a condition which was aggravated by supplementary feeding of the sheep especially in the winter so creating localised areas of extreme grazing and trampling. The National Trust had no power to control sheep numbers but with the assistance of the Long Mynd Commoners'

Gorse and heather topiary caused by sheep eating the tender new shoots; sheep can only reach so far!

Association, English Nature and Defra, a phased reduction over a period of years has been agreed.

Sheep have surprisingly discerning palates and do not simply munch their way indiscriminately across

Three fine Shropshire yearling rams bred in the 1920s by Joseph Lockhart, a Culmington farmer. They display the woolly face and fleece then demanded by the international market but later bred out. Mr Edwards, the shepherd (with his son) holds a leg crook, the time-honoured way of catching individual sheep.

the hillsides but target those areas of nutrient-rich vegetation which reflects that of the underlying soil and is greatest over nutrient-rich rock. Tree seedlings are the first to be eaten since they are both nutritious and inherently exposed. The consequence is that sustained grazing gradually eliminates woodland by preventing natural regeneration. Heather and other small shrubs are the next to be eaten because of their tasty new growth coming from the dividing tissues at the shoot tips. Grasses and sedges have adapted to resist grazing because their tender new growth is tucked away at ground level and difficult to reach.

Welsh Mountain ewe and lamb.

Sheep Breeds

The fleeces from Shropshire's indigenous sheep in the fourteenth century were the most highly prized in the whole country. These sheep, the so-called 'Shropshire old sheep' or 'Longmynd', were described in 1803 as nimble, hardy and horned with a face colour ranging from black through brown to speckled and they yielded 2–2½ lb of quality wool. In the early 1800s, experiments in cross breeding were carried out to improve the stock and it was found that Southdown ram crosses with the Longmynd ewes improved the wool and carcass weight. By 1859, this new cross called 'Shropshires' had been established and registered as a distinct breed and produced a fleece weighing 5–8 lb. Their adaptability to all kinds of pasture land, hardiness to withstand our variable climate, close, oily wool to shield them from the snows and sleet and their longevity and prolificacy made them widely popular and were exported worldwide.

The original Longmynd breed continued but became extinct in 1926. Nowadays, the Shropshire breed which grazed on the Long Mynd have been replaced by the Welsh Mountain breed of sheep.

Hefted sheep

The extensive grazing of hefted sheep on the common land of Britain is a unique phenomenon in Europe, enabling livestock to be kept in unfenced areas without constant shepherding. Each hefted flock has its own territory and is self-confining to that area, a heft, with each flock knowing its own area.

Each family of sheep, a ewe and her daughters over several generations, stay together as a small group within the flock and the whole flock grazes one area so that the entire common or moor is a mosaic of different hefted flocks. Genetic material is introduced by selected rams but the matriarchal lineage is not interrupted.

A hefted ewe possesses knowledge that she teaches to her lambs. They need to know where to graze and find nutritional benefits such as the protein-rich new shoots of cotton grass, where streams or bogs may be safely crossed, where to go in different weather and at times of day or night to find shelter, shade or safety.

Each ewe in a flock is identified by various coloured marks on her shoulder, back or leg and a characteristic shaped notch in one or both ears as well as the two statutory ear tags.

Hebridean Sheep

Hebridean sheep are an ideal breed for clearing rough ground and they readily eat brambles, nettles, docks and saplings. They are a browser as well as a grazer, that is, they will nibble trees and foliage and not just expect lush fertile grass. In this way they mimic the old fashioned breeds that grazed pastures and helped to create and maintain them; modern breeds of sheep prefer swards of improved grass! The National Trust owns a flock of Hebrideans and uses them mostly for clearing the land on Wenlock Edge. They can be seen in The Batch during the winter months where they are given a rest and change of diet.

Hebridean sheep are described as nimble, an understatement since they are not easy to herd nor catch.

Ponies

For centuries sheep shared the Long Mynd with cattle and horses and by the late 17th century most husbandmen's livestock included one or two mares and colts. A few of the wealthier commoners were breeding and rearing large numbers of horses and ponies on the common. Now there is a limit of thirty ponies (plus foals under two years old) on the Long Mynd, all owned by one farmer.

Ponies had been bred on the Long Mynd since the 12th century for use as packhorses along the Portway. The boom in industrial activity during the late 18th century increased the demand for ponies. A further boost came in 1842 when the Mines Act prohibited women from hauling coal in the pits and ponies took over the work. In 1890, the Long Mynd Hill Pony Improvement Association was formed to eliminate substandard stallions.

Because of their small size (less than 12 hands), the Welsh Mountain pony was used in the South Wales coal mines. They are reputed to be trustworthy,

Welsh Mountain pony and foal.

of a good disposition with even temperament and friendly character but spirited and with great endurance. They are known for their stamina, soundness and high level of intelligence which usually makes them easy to train.

With the closure of most of the Welsh pits by the 1990s, many of the ponies were taken to the Long Mynd and most of the present stock are their descendents. The breed comes in a range of colours and those on the Long Mynd, the Cwmdale lineage, are mostly brown or white with each family group being of same colour.

Ponies' hooves had kept the hills free of bracken allowing grass to grow, not only for themselves but also for sheep. Their absence may have resulted in a rapid spread of bracken over the common land.

Cattle

Besides sheep and ponies, cattle have always been grazed on the Long Mynd. In the 17th and 18th centuries bullocks of the Hereford type were grazed on the Long Mynd to be sold on to be fattened elsewhere. As the moor was being developed as a shooting estate, the few cattle on it were held responsible for the damage done to the shooting butts that had been constructed and the commoners were discouraged from putting cattle on the moor.

The Church Stretton pony and sheep sales were held at the corner of Burway Road and Longhills Road after the Market Square and High Street became too crowded. The horses and ponies wearing only halters are likely to have been the ones for sale. A 1905 photograph.

Cultivation

The Ratlinghope manorial court record of 1698 mentions ploughing and intermittent cultivation of waste land on the Long Mynd. Peat (known then as turf) was also cut for fuel although there are only small deposits of peat on the hill. The same record also mentions that parishioners of Church Stretton had cut turf stealthily which suggests that only tenants of Rarlinghope held turbary, the right to cut peat. Ling was regularly cut and is still occasionally used for fuel and low quality thatch.

Markets and Fairs

THE IMPORTANCE of sheep, horses and cattle at Church Stretton markets and fairs reflected the predominantly pastoral economy of the area. It was, however, sheep and ponies which provided the majority of animals at the fairs. Fair days included the statute fair (14th May) when sheep and lambs were sorted and sold; the wool fair on 3rd June; the great sheep and colt fair on 25th September, and deadman's fair on the last Thursday of November.

Seeing the potential to make some money, a decree of 1629 allowed Thomas Thynne, the lord of the manor of Stretton-en-le-Dale, to take a toll on all kinds of corn and grain, all horses, geldings, oxen, bullocks, cows, heifers, sheep, hogs and other cattle.

Livestock sales in Church Stretton were originally held in the town's main street, originally called Bristol Road and now called High Street. This wide space soon became too crowded to house the large numbers of sheep and ponies brought for sale and the market was moved to the foot of Burway Road on the green near Longhills Road; even so, it often extended down to Shrewsbury Road. With the advent of the motor car and increased traffic levels, the sheep fair was moved again to Lion Meadow until that finally closed about 1982. As demand for pit ponies fell, the old horse fairs declined in importance and eventually stopped.

The various packhorse trails and drover's routes across the Long Mynd, together with the Portway itself, bears witness to the importance of these routes linking outlying villages with the markets at Shrewsbury, Church Stretton, Clun and Bishop's Castle. Indeed, the Portway became particularly popular when the road through the Stretton gap was turnpiked in 1756, but it's use declined rapidly after the building of the Shrewsbury–Hereford railway line in 1852.

The pony and sheep sales in Church Stretton were a popular event which stretched down Burway Road as far as the junction with High Street and Shrewsbury Road. Photo about 1900.

© Tony Crowe Collection

Traffic congestion forced the Church Stretton sheep sales to be moved to Sheep Sales Field (Lion Meadow) shown here. It continued here until about 1982. Even so, it was a common sight to see animals being driven through the town.

Prior to the industrial revolution the economy of Britain grew on the backs of sheep. They were valued for their milk which was made into cheese, their skins for parchment and their wool for cloth.

Horses and ponies being brought down from the Long Mynd to Inwood, September 1906.

Now, only about 30 ponies graze on the Long Mynd.

Kestrel

Long Mynd Birds

BIRDS ADD so much to a walk on the Long Mynd; there is every chance of seeing buzzards, ravens, skylarks, pipits, stonechats, whinchats, grey wagtails, red grouse and kestrels in addition to the ubiquitous crows and rooks on the lower slopes. Birds are most active and feeding during the early and later parts of the day and so these are the best times to see them.

In order for the smaller upland birds to reduce the risk of predation they have evolved a range of adaptations which even out the contest between hunter and hunted. Most, and especially the females, are a dull colour to avoid detection by blending with their surroundings. Losses by predation are made up through higher breeding rates with the result that predators and prey tend to stay roughly in equilibrium.

So as to maximise their lifetime reproductive output, small birds tend to 'live fast, die young' and lay many eggs or have several clutches each year. The larger birds, though, tend to be longer lived and rear few, if any, young in one year but have a long reproductive life. Over their lifetimes, any pair of birds only needs to rear two young to maturity to replace themselves.

Nest site availability and food supply are key factors in determining what sort of bird and how many may live on the Long Mynd. Small birds who rely on insects and seeds can occur at relatively high densities with hundreds of pairs of meadow pipits per square kilometre, while the prey of carnivores (buzzards, ravens, peregrines, red kites) is relatively scarce, so each pair will defend a large area to provide all their needs. For buzzards, a pair may need an area of several square kilometres.

Some upland bird species require areas of short, cropped grassland in which to feed. However, this type of turf does not usually provide enough cover for skylarks or other ground-nesting birds to breed. Upland field boundaries, where they occur, are usually fences and any hedges tend to consist only of scattered relict hawthorns giving little protection for nesting birds. Upland pasture therefore tends to be used by birds for feeding rather than breeding. Carrion-feeding birds such as buzzards, crows and ravens are particularly numerous on these areas of grassland.

Sheep carcasses are an abundant food source in all seasons, especially during winter. They were at one time collected and sold to knackers' yards but this was banned during the outbreak of BSE in the early 1990s. Defra and English Nature still require the removal of carcasses but there is no incentive for farmers to do this and so it often does not happen.

The Long Mynd is probably the most important area for birds in the West Midlands, lying on the boundary between the wild uplands of the Welsh hills and the lowland agricultural plains of Cheshire and the West Midlands. Numbers can vary considerably from year to year depending on the weather and food availability during the winter for resident birds and similarly for migrants whilst abroad.

The birds described on the following pages are far from a complete list but are a selection of the more interesting or unusual birds that inhabit the plateau and valleys. Many of the birds are on the red or amber list of birds of national conservation concern. The description 'Long Mynd, very high priority' or 'high priority' refers to the local National Trust priority for conservation management.

© Richard Warren

Grey wagtails often nest in the Light Spout Hollow.

Red Kite

RED KITES are the most graceful of Britain's birds of prey. Currently, they are being seen more frequently on the western and southern slopes of the Long Mynd and in the Stretton valley. They are easily recognised by their forked tail and striking colour, predominantly chestnut red with white patches under the wings. Against the light, the tail looks almost a translucent brick-red colour. They are incredibly agile and twist and turn like a child's kite when foraging quite low above fields.

Red kites are slightly larger than buzzards and have a much longer, though narrower, wingspan. They have a relatively small body weight of 2–3 lbs which makes them more buoyant.

Until some 200 years ago the red kite was a common British bird seen almost anywhere in the country from Scotland to the streets of London. However, in the late 18th and 19th centuries their numbers were drastically reduced. Improvements in hygiene in towns and cities reduced carrion and human waste as a ready source of food and the establishment of game estates for pheasants and rabbits meant that predatory animals and birds were viewed as vermin. Thus red kites were simultaneously starved out of towns and shot or poisoned in the countryside.

Numbers were down to only three females in Wales in 1900. By the 1930s their population had risen to 11 pairs in remote oak woods of central Wales but numbers slowly increased to a hundred pairs in the mid 1990s as a result of conservation measures. From 1989, a reintroduction programme to release birds from Spain and Sweden to parts of England and Scotland has been very successful and has introduced a fresh genetic pool. The bird's territorial expansion into more fertile lowland areas has meant that different populations are now overlapping and interbreeding. The Welsh population has now expanded into the Marches and is now over a thousand breeding pairs with 20 nests found and 35 young fledged in 2011 in South Shropshire, the best year so far. They are on the national amber list.

They nest in trees making use of old buzzard or raven nests which they refurbish with wool interwoven with old rags, paper and plastic found from human settlements. The vagabond Autolycus in *The Winter's Tale* warns 'when the kite builds, look to your lesser

> The UK's leading bird conservation organisations list birds according to their level of conservation concern:
> Red: Severe decline in range and population of both breeding and non-breeding birds.
> Amber: Moderate decline in range and population of both breeding and non-breeding birds.
> Green: No concern.

linen'. Kites probably did snatch the odd item from clothes lines!

The red kite is primarily a scavenger and an opportunist. They profit from sheep carrion but are not capable of opening up carcasses by themselves and have to wait until more powerful birds such as ravens or buzzards have made the first inroads before it will attempt to feed. They also take a wide variety of live prey ranging from earthworms to small mammals, amphibians and birds.

The word kite probably stems from the old English *cyta* meaning a bird of prey of the hawk family and distinguished by long pointed wings and a forked tail. The bird was also called a *glade* in England during the Middle Ages. The toy kite was so called in the 1660s from its way of hovering in the air like the kite.

Merlin

Close or prolonged views of merlins are a rare event to the casual observer and often the best that can be hoped for is a fleeting glimpse as the bird flashes past just above the heather on the Long Mynd plateau. They have a fast, low, direct flight and twist and turn when chasing their prey. Merlins may be seen hunting over any part of the heather heathland until May when the female sits tight on her nest. The best time to see them is in July after the young have fledged.

Only one or two pairs of merlins nest each year on the Long Mynd in old crows nests in old hawthorn trees on the steep hillsides. Their chief prey is the meadow pipit but they eat a wide range of species and need some 450 small birds to sustain a pair through the breeding season. Thus the limitation in their numbers is the availability of small birds which in turn is dependent upon the relative amount of grass and heather. They also eat moths and beetles. Merlins are on the national amber list (Long Mynd, very high priority).

© Hilary Chambers

Merlins are Britain's smallest bird of prey and are about the size of a blackbird, the males having a light blue-grey back and wing and a buff-orange breast with dark streaks whilst the females are dark brown above.

Like all birds of prey, their numbers were decimated by the use of chemical pesticides and persecution by gamekeepers, though this was unjustified because merlins are hunters taking small birds as they fly, especially meadow pipits, rather than game-bird chicks on the ground.

The merlin is an important falconry species. It was referred to as the ladies' hawk because it was lighter on the wrist. Around the 1900s, skylarks were kept in captivity specially for hawking. When both were released they would rise ever higher in the sky almost out of sight before the merlin caught its prey and return to earth at great speed.

The name merlin originates from the 14th century Anglo-French *merilun*, itself based on the old French *esmerillon*. There does not seem to be any connection with the Merlin of Arthurian legend. The bird has become synonymous with speed despite its faster flying relative, the peregrine; after all, the Spitfire aeroplane was powered by the Rolls Royce Merlin engine, not the Peregrine engine!

Raven

R AVENS ARE a common sight on and around the Long Mynd nowadays. A hundred years ago, they were absent after their last nest was robbed in1884, not to reappear again until 1918. Since then, there has been a very slow comeback.

Often it is their distinctive deep 'cronk' call that alerts one to look upwards to see a pair wheeling and soaring together high above. They are mighty birds, half as big again as a crow and the size of a buzzard and are completely black, including their massive beak. In flight their wedge-shaped tail is a characteristic feature. They are a long-lived bird and typically live for 10–15 years and up to 40 years in captivity. They build enormous nests of twigs wedged in a forked branch high up in a conifer tree.

Big, Bold and Black

Due to their size, gregariousness and defensive abilities, ravens have few natural predators other than man. They eat mainly carrion and their population growth is largely due to the increase of it left lying around the hills. Sheep carcasses used to be taken to the knacker's yard but the financial incentive for this disappeared when the government changed the regulations governing the use of material reclaimed from carrion to combat the spread of BSE in the 1990s.

It is hard to imagine that a completely black bird could possess so much character. With their satanic look, they feature extensively in mythology and literature and feature in half of Shakespeare's plays, normally as a portent of doom, a role quite befitting a carrion feeder with such a close interest in death. In the bible, the raven features in 12 verses and was the first animal to be released from Noah's ark. A legend developed that England would not fall to a foreign invader so long as there were ravens at the Tower of London. Although this is often thought to be an ancient belief, it is actually a romantic Victorian invention.

The brains of ravens count among the largest of any bird species and appear to display ability in problem solving as well as other cognitive processes such as imitation and insight.

One experiment designed to evaluate insight and problem solving ability involved a piece of meat attached to a string hanging from a perch. To reach the food, the bird needed to stand on the perch, pull the string up a little at a time and step on the loops to gradually shorten the string with no demonstrable trial and error learning. This supports the notion that ravens have the ability to solve problems presented to them. It is becoming clear that ravens are actually very intelligent.

Their name dates back directly to the language spoken by the Anglo-Saxons when they were called the *hrafn*. Odin, the war god of Norse legend was known as *hrafnagud*, the raven god. Two ravens were his eyes and ears and flew across the world collecting information and returned to perch on each shoulder and whispered to him everything that was happening.

Local historic evidence for ravens lies in the seven field names in the east end of Ashes Hollow in Little Stretton each of which incorporates the name raven.

Common Buzzard

BUZZARDS ARE the most common of the large birds of prey likely to be seen in Shropshire. A pair may often be seen soaring above the valleys and batches of the Long Mynd as well as over the Church Stretton valley. In the late summer, they may be seen with one or two young in a family party soaring effortlessly on rising thermals and one's attention may be drawn to them first by their penetrating cat-like '*mewing*' call. Whilst soaring they are frequently mobbed by other birds, particularly crows and ravens. Soaring is a territorial display, though when watching such a graceful display, one cannot help get the feeling that the birds are thoroughly enjoying the experience.

Buzzards are large birds but not as big as red kites or ravens which are the three local large predators or scavengers. Their plumage can vary considerably with patterns of predominantly brown but with added black, grey and white. They almost always have a large pale or white area under their particularly broad wings which makes them easily recognisable.

Buzzards nest in mature deciduous trees located mainly in nearby woods and isolated trees around the edge of the Long Mynd and in the upper reaches of secluded valleys. There are about 20 breeding pairs (in addition to immature and unpaired birds) in neighbouring woods and hills which include the Long Mynd in their hunting area. Their main food is young rabbits and voles but in the winter they will eat sheep carrion and worms but rarely grouse or partridges. They are often seen perching on telegraph poles or other prominent perch where they can scan the vicinity for small prey. They regularly allow a close approach before flying off.

Until thirty years ago, buzzards were quite rare because of persecution from gamekeepers and, to a lesser extent, farmers. The population was decimated by the myxomatosis epidemic of the 1950s which killed their main food source, rabbits. Since then, they have benefitted from a much enlightened attitude to persecution and conservation and an improved food supply of sheep carrion and rabbits as the latter slowly increased in number after the myxomatosis epidemic. The recovery of the buzzard population is undoubtedly a successful conservation story.

In Britain, they were originally called *tysca*. The name buzzard comes from the medieval French *busard*. Now, they are officially called the common buzzard.

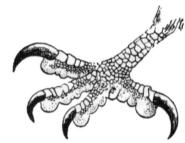

The powerful foot of a buzzard has strong, long claws for killing mammals.

Peregrine Falcon

Peregrine falcons have made a remarkable comeback in recent years after their devastation by the now-banned organochlorine pesticides. They may be seen soaring or floating in the wind in the spring or summer months. They feed mainly on medium sized birds, especially pigeons and if you are lucky you may see one dive with folded-back wings at great speed onto an unsuspecting victim, catching it in mid air. They are the ultimate aerial predators and are superbly adapted with acute eyesight, strong legs and sharp talons to grip its prey. They are the fastest of all birds and have been recorded diving at speeds up to 150 mph, though speeds half that are more usual. When pulling out of a dive they experience a positive force of 25 G; humans lose consciousness if subjected to a force of 9 G without special suits.

Peregrines are about the size of a crow. They have a blue-grey back and upper wings, a white breast with horizontal finely spotted or barred streaks and their face is white with a prominent black moustache. They prefer rocky areas and cliffs on which they build their nest and may be seen at the southern end of the Long Mynd. They are on the national amber list.

Feral pigeons are their favourite prey wherever they are freely available though a wide range of other birds are taken, ranging in size from goldcrest to grey heron. The larger females take larger prey than males. Their generalist diet allows them to exist wherever there are good mixed bird populations. They sometimes take mammals and there are records of occasional amphibians, lizards and large insects being taken as well.

Like all birds of prey, they have been the subject of much persecution and there is still hostility from pigeon fanciers who mistakenly believe that they are responsible for the high mortality among racing pigeons. The Raptor Study Group reported that only 7.5% of homing pigeons were killed by raptors out of the 52% that failed to return home, the rest being killed by flying into pylons or losing their way.

Falconry, 1250.

Historically, falconry was a popular sport and status symbol among the nobles of medieval Europe, the Middle East and Mongolian Empire. Peregrine falcons are still the top choice for falconry by kings and nobles, particularly in Arab countries. In art and in other aspects of culture such as literature, falconry remained a status symbol long after it was no longer popularly practiced. The Bayeux Tapestry shows King Harold with a hawk in one scene. It is said that the King owned the largest collection of books on the sport in all of Europe. The popularity of falconry and the high price offered for birds and their eggs means that there is much illegal trapping and thieving. Nowadays, British falconers are entirely reliant upon captive-bred birds for their sport.

The name peregrine derives from old French *faulcon pelerin* and the latin *falco peregrinus* of the 13th century meaning a wandering falcon.

Kestrel

© Hilary Chambers

They often catch several voles in succession and cache some for later. The stored food is usually eaten the same day just before dusk. This reduces the risk that the bird would have to go to roost on an empty stomach.

In the 1950s kestrels were becoming increasingly rare having been persecuted by gamekeepers for decades, falsely being accused of taking young game birds. Thousands of birds had been poisoned by DDT and other powerful agricultural pesticides which had been used for many years but once their use had been banned, the numbers of kestrels started to recover. They are, nevertheless, very susceptible to the periodic population changes of field voles which rise and crash every four years or so. There are usually around 5 pairs which hunt on the Long Mynd. Kestrels are on the national amber list.

The name originates from the 15th century *castrell* a derivation of the Old French *crecele* meaning a rattle, alluding to its *kee kee kee* call.

KESTRELS ARE readily recognised when they hover over the grassy banks of motorways and other roads. Once called the windhover, they appear almost stationary as they hover with their head down facing into the wind seeking the tell-tale movements of a vole or mouse in the grass below. With their keen eyesight, sharp talons and strong beak, kestrels are well adapted to catching small agile prey. They are colourful birds about the same size as a jackdaw. The male has a blue-grey head and tail, buff-brown speckled underparts, bronze-coloured back and pointed wings which have a black tip.

On the Long Mynd, their favourite hunting areas are the edges of heathland where there is short vegetation at the top of steep banks which combine the habitat of field voles with up-draughts of air so that they can see, hover and descend upon their food. Their most common prey is the short-tailed field vole which is supplemented by other small mammals such as wood mice and shrews as well as insects, earthworms and small birds.

Kestrels are capable of locating their prey at remarkable distances; they can see and catch a beetle 50 m from their perch. Kestrels need to eat 4–8 voles a day, depending on the time of the year and the amount of energy-consuming hover-hunting they do.

© Christine Matthews

Sparrowhawk

FOR MANY people the first awareness of a sparrowhawk is of one flashing past above a hedge or wall accompanied by the panic alarm calls and scattering of small birds. Sparrowhawks are adept hunters and depend on surprising their prey and snatching it in flight. They typically fly low at breakneck speed along lanes and suddenly turn off skimming along a hedge and disappearing onto the other side. They are well adapted for hunting birds in confined spaces like woodland and gardens, though they are not built for stamina and long chases. They can fly faster than blue tits and sparrows but not as fast as chaffinches, blackbirds and starlings so their hunting technique largely relies on an element of surprise. A hunting sparrowhawk can be so focussed on its task that

it can put itself at risk of harm from collisions. Because they are quite easily seen, small birds will give warning calls to each other and only about one attack in ten results in capture. They have learnt that gardens are an easy source of prey, bringing the realities of nature up close to our homes and have been nicknamed 'the garden terrorist'.

Male sparrowhawks are about the same size as kestrels; the females being larger than males, as with most birds of prey. In flight the overall impression of the sparrowhawk is grey with broad wings. Adult male sparrowhawks have bluish-grey back and wings and orangey-brown bars on their chest. Females and young birds have brown back and wings, and brown bars underneath. They have bright yellow-orange eyes, long yellow legs and long talons.

Because of their preference for woodland, they are only seen in those wooded valleys of the Long Mynd such as the lower reaches of Ashes Hollow, Callow Hollow, Carding Mill Valley, Stanbatch and The Batch at All Stretton.

In 1696, John Aubrey wrote 'Not long before the death of King Charles II a sparrowhawk escaped from the perch and pitched on one of the iron crowns of the White Tower and, entangling its string in the crown, hung by the heels and died. 'Twas considered very ominous and so it proved'

The male sparrowhawk is named a 'musket' in falconry and the early muzzle-loading long gun used by infantry was named a musket because of it's popularity with hunters.

Skylark

© Hilary Chambers

THE SKYLARK is the classic bird of moorland, hovering at great heights and singing away for all its worth. The skylark is renowned for its song flight, the male bird rises vertically from the ground high into the air where it remains stationary for several minutes on fluttering wings before dropping back down to the ground. The length of time it stays aloft and sings is an indication to its mate of how good a father he will be and a warning to other males that this is his territory. All the time it is in the air the bird continuously sings its heart out with its liquid warbling song. It is not surprising that the collective name for skylarks is an 'exaltation'.

Skylarks are restricted to the Long Mynd plateau where there are up to 200 nesting pairs in a good year. They are somewhat larger than a sparrow but smaller than a starling. They have brown upper parts and a paler streaked breast and a characteristic small crest which can sometimes be seen when they are on the ground. They prefer a habitat where there is an open mixture of bracken, heather, bilberry and grass. Their camouflaged nest is difficult to find; it is built on the ground and usually hidden by a tussock of grass or heather. They typically lay 3–5 eggs and often have a second brood. In the winter they move to lower pastures.

The national decline in the skylark population, caused mainly by lowland farming activities, makes the management of their Long Mynd habitat a high priority in order to maintain their high breeding density here. Skylarks are on the national red list (Long Mynd, high priority).

Formerly, skylarks and wheatears were eaten in large numbers; 300 skylarks were made into a pie to celebrate the opening of the Forth Railway Bridge in 1890!

The popularity of the skylark is shown by it frequently being the subject of poetry, music and song. *To a Skylark* by William Wordsworth is perhaps the most apt:

> *Up with me! up with me into the clouds!*
> *For thy song, Lark, is strong;*
> *Up with me, up with me into the clouds!*
> *Singing, singing,*
> *With clouds and sky about thee ringing,*
> *Lift me, guide me till I find*
> *That spot which seems so to thy mind!*

The popular children's round *Alouette* is not really a very nice song since the words inform the lark that the singer will pluck its head, nose, eyes and wings and tail:

> *Alouette, gentille Alouette*
> *Alouette je te plumerai*
> *Je te plumerai la tête, etc.*

The beautiful *Lark Ascending* is a work by the English composer Ralph Vaughan Williams, inspired by George Meredith's poem about the skylark. It is one of the most popular pieces in the classical repertoire among British listeners.

Larks, like other singing birds were prized as cage birds.

Pipits

They are the same size as a sparrow and have a longish tail. Meadow pipits are very common and probably outnumber all other bird species on the Long Mynd, it being the home to over a thousand pairs. Unfortunately for them, they are the merlin's favourite food.

The characteristic aerial display of pipits allows them to be told apart. The meadow pipit starts its performance on the plateau from the ground and flutters vertically into the air with a jerky flight before 'parachuting' down with wings held still and outspread to where it started. Throughout the entire flight it keeps up a twittering song. The tree pipit does the same but generally from the branch of a tree on the hillsides, finishing its song with *zeeah, zeeah, zeeah.*

THE MEADOW PIPIT and the tree pipit are almost impossible to tell apart. They are the definitive 'little brown bird' of the moorland, brown above and pale and speckled below with white outer tail feathers. They are, though, very engaging little birds.

> *It's a pity pipits have*
> *No diagnostic features*
> *Specifically they are the least*
> *Distinctive of God's creatures*

Their nest is usually woven into a tuft of rough grass. They usually have two clutches of 4–5 eggs. During the winter, the meadow pipit moves to lower ground whilst the tree pipit usually migrates to southern Europe. Both tree pipits and meadow pipits are on the national amber list (Long Mynd, very high priority).

The cuckoo often lays its eggs in the nest of the meadow pipit whose name in Welsh is *gwas-y-gog*, meaning cuckoo's servant.

The typical habitat of meadow pipits.

Dipper

© Northeastwildlife.co.uk

DIPPERS ARE plump little birds related to the wren. They are bigger than a robin and have black backs, a dazzling white throat, a chestnut belly and have noticeably short tails. They are delightful residents of fast flowing streams often first noticed by their sharp '*chink*' call given in flight as they fly very close to the surface of the water to the end of their territory before they fly back to allow you a second look. They often are seen bobbing on a rock in the stream before they hop into the water where they walk about on the stream bed overturning stones to feed on invertebrates such as mayfly nymphs, caddis fly larvae, snails, fresh water shrimps and small fish such as bullheads and trout fry They can use their short powerful wings as flippers under water and give the impression of flying beneath the surface. Their strong legs and claws allow them to grip rocks on the river bed. Dippers can find aquatic invertebrates in rivers even in mid-winter, feeding briefly under a surface covering of ice when necessary.

They build their nests among tree roots on the stream bank and on ledges or in cracks under bridges. Unfortunately it is now several years since they have nested in the Carding Mill Valley. A nest box project on the Clun and Onny rivers has increased their population there.

Dippers are vulnerable to changes in the streams such as low water levels, their purity and acidity which reduces the invertebrates population. Populations usually are able to recover when the conditions improve.

© Northeastwildlife.co.uk

Wheatears, Whinchats and Stonechats

THESE ARE the typical birds of the upper slopes of the valleys radiating out from the Long Mynd plateau. They are spring and summer migrants, though a few stonechats over-winter except in periods of prolonged frost or snow. They are all insect eating birds, about the size of a robin.

Wheatear

Wheatear

WHEATEARS are the first of the summer migrants to arrive and are found on rocky hillsides where there is short grass, poor soil or scree and where they can make their nest in a rabbit burrow or rock crevice. They may also be found in the vicinity of the glider field. Wheatears often perch prominently on nearby rocky outcrops or boulders. Male birds are unmistakable being blue-grey above, black wings and white below with a sandy coloured breast and a bold black stripe through the eye. The female is brown but both sexes show a prominent white rump in flight. (Long Mynd, very high priority).

In Victorian times, roasted wheatears were highly recommended although the size of the birds meant that it was always considered a delicacy. Mrs Beaton gave a recipe for them, helpfully noting that they are seasonal from July to October! Their name derives from the Middle English 'white arse' alluding to their flashy white rump.

Stonechat

STONECHATS are the resident equivalent of whinchats though some young migrate in the winter. They are mainly found on steep heathery slopes and plateau near bracken or gorse and typically perch on prominent rocks or bushes. Males are colourful birds with black heads, white around the side of their neck, orange-red breasts and a mottled brown back. Females lack the male's black head but have brown backs and an orange tinge to their chests. Both have white wing bars which are particularly noticeable in flight. Often it is a sharp loud *tac-tac* call that sounds like two stones being tapped together that draws them to one's attention and which gives them their name. Stonechats are on the national amber list but have increased in recent mild winters (Long Mynd, very high priority).

Stonechat

Whinchat

WHINCHATS are summer visitors and a duller version of stonechats. They have streaky brown head and backs, a prominent white eye-stripe, buff-coloured breast and white outer tail feathers. Again, they inhabit the upper reaches of all the valleys and sing from a prominent sprig of heather or bracken. They get their name from *whin* which is an old name for bracken which seems to be their traditional habitat. Whinchats are only found on steep hillsides with bracken and the National Trust is managing the bracken on hillsides with whinchats in mind. (Long Mynd, very high priority).

Of these three birds, there are perhaps about 60 pairs of whinchats, 40 pairs of stonechats and 30 pairs of wheatears on the Long Mynd. In general, numbers of whinchat and wheatear are declining while numbers of stonechat were increasing until the bad winter of 2012.

Whinchat

© Northeastwildlife.co.uk

© Frank Vassen

Reed bunting

REED BUNTINGS are entirely dependent on the wet flush habitat that surrounds the springs and pools on the Long Mynd. The best place to see them is in the vegetation surrounding Wildmoor Pool. Although they are resident birds in Britain, most leave the Long Mynd in September, not returning again until the following May to breed. They are the size of a sparrow, albeit slimmer; the male in summer plumage is unmistakable and handsome with a black head and bib and with an obvious white collar and underparts. The female is, as usual, duller with a brown streaky head and less obvious collar. Locally, they are called reed sparrow. They are on the national amber list (Long Mynd, very high priority).

Reed beds in a Long Mynd pool, an ideal habitat for reed bumtings.

Wagtails

BOTH THE grey wagtail and the pied wagtail are to be found in or near the lower reaches of fast flowing streams in the Long Mynd valleys. Their body is intermediate in size between a sparrow and a starling; they are easily recognised by their very long slender tail which they flick up and down. Wagtails are dainty, graceful birds.

Grey Wagtail

© Northeastwildlife.co.uk

THE NAME of the grey wagtail is a bit of a misnomer since the first thing you see is its bright yellow underside. They have a pale grey back, head and tail, and a white eye-stripe. They may be seen foraging in the stream and on the bank and adjacent trees seeking larvae, insects and caterpillars. Unlike dippers, they are less vulnerable to changes in the stream level. They nest in crevices in nearby rock outcrops and will even nest on buildings. There are about six pairs of grey wagtails nesting in the Long Mynd valleys. They are on the national amber list (Long Mynd, high priority).

Pied Wagtail

THIS BIRD is entirely black and white with a white face and black bib. When not standing and frantically wagging its tail up and down it can be seen dashing about over stretches of short grass or car parks in search of food. They can nest away from streams on buildings and derelict sites. On the Long Mynd, they regularly nest at Pole Cottage and the glider station. Their numbers are about the same as for their grey wagtail cousins.

© Northeastwildlife.co.uk

John Clare's poem *Little Trotty Wagtail* beautifully describes its behaviour:

Little trotty wagtail he went in the rain,
And tittering, tottering sideways he neer
*   got straight again,*
He stooped to get a worm, and looked up to get a fly,
And then he flew away ere his feathers they were dry.

Little trotty wagtail, he waddled in the mud,
And left his little footmarks, trample where he would.
He waddled in the water-pudge, and waggle went his
*   tail,*
And chirrup up his wings to dry upon the garden rail.

Little trotty wagtail, you nimble all about,
And in the dimpling water-pudge you waddle in and out;
Your home is nigh at hand, and in the warm pig-stye,
So, little Master Wagtail, I'll bid you a good-bye.

Fieldfares, Redwings and Mistle Thrushes

THE SIGHT of fieldfares and redwings can make a cold winter's walk a delight. Sometimes large flocks of these birds come to the Long Mynd during periods of harsh weather in Northern Europe and Scandinavia. They fly in on an easterly wind because their usual food supply is closing down for the winter. Our berries will fuel them up again for their great push south to winter in Southern Europe, North Africa and Turkey. They may be seen anywhere from the plateau to the valley bottom where they travel in flocks scavenging the remaining berries on hawthorn, rowan and other fruit-bearing trees and shrubs. Mistle thrushes are of the same family but are resident all the year round.

Fieldfare

FIELDFARES are larger than the common song thrush. They are colourful birds with a chestnut brown back, grey head and rump and a heavily spotted cream-coloured chest and white belly. They are noisy birds and make a loud chuckling sound as they feed. They are on the national amber list.

Typically seen on frosty winter days, Chaucer described them as 'frosty fieldfares' and John Clare summed them up in his *The Shepherd's Calendar:*

> *Flocking fieldfares, speckled like the thrush,*
> *Picking the red haw from the sweeing bush*
> *That come and go one winters chilling wing*
> *And seem to share no sympathy with spring.*

© Hilary Chambers

Fieldfare

Mistle Thrush

MISTLE THRUSHES breed in trees in many of the valleys. They are paler than their over-wintering relatives and have large black speckles on their chest and belly. They give the impression of being aggressive and powerful as they stand very upright. Besides berries, they eat worms, slugs and insects. In the autumn, they tend to move around in flocks on the Long Mynd feeding on bilberries and rowan berries. On the plateau, they can be easily confused with merlins. Mistle thrushes nest in the forks of substantial trees in early March usually before the leaves come out. They are on the national amber list.

They get their name from a supposed liking for mistletoe berries, though these constitute only a tiny part of their diet. They are also known as 'storm cocks' because of their habit of sitting high in a tree singing loudly during stormy weather when other birds find shelter.

Redwing

REDWINGS are smaller than fieldfares and about the size of a song thrush. They have a prominent creamy white eye-stripe and their underwings and flanks are red which is clearly visible and characteristic when flying. They, too, make a chattering or chuckling call. They are on the amber list.

© Kev Chapman

© Hilary Chambers

Mistle Thrush with a beak full of caterpillars.

Grasshopper Warbler

This skulking warbler is rarely seen and easily overlooked until its song is heard. Its call is remarkably like a stridulating grasshopper or cricket and may be heard at dawn or dusk at the top of Ashes Hollow or on Wildmoor where there is open land with thick vegetation and scattered bushes. It is a very secretive bird which is declining nationally but on the Long Mynd there is a welcome increase with several pairs regularly breeding.

Yellowhammer

A YELLOWHAMMER cannot be mistaken for any other bird; its yellow colour stands out as it sings from a prominent perch with its distinctive rhythmic lilt often described as '*a-little-bit-of-bread-and-nooo-cheese*'. Their yellow head and breast has brown streaks and their back and tail is predominantly streaky brown. Their habitat in the Long Mynd valleys comprises areas where there are trees, gorse, bracken and grass. They nest on or near the ground and use the trees as song posts and sources for food. They are on the national red list.

Andrew Young describes their behaviour in his poem:

> *Yellow-hammers, gold-headed, russet-backed,*
> *They fled in jerky flight before my feet,*
> *Or pecked in the green ranks of winter wheat,*
> *While I my footsteps slacked.*

Redstart

Redstarts are common summer visitors to the Long Mynd having wintered in West Africa. The males are handsome brightly coloured birds with an orange-red breast, rust-red tail, slate-grey upper parts, black face and a white forehead. They are about the size of a robin. The females are basically brown but have the same red tail. When the bird is flying away from the observer, it is the red tail that first catches the eye and confirms identification.

They nest in holes in older trees, especially hawthorns and so they are most likely to be found on the steep valley sides where there are such trees. They feed on the insects and larvae in the foliage of the trees and also in the short grass beneath. Over a hundred pairs breed within the National Trust boundary and many more on other parts of the Long Mynd. They are on the national amber list (Long Mynd, high priority).

The name redstart literally means red tail, the 'start' coming from the Old English *steort*, meaning tail. The old Shropshire name for it is fiery brantail.

Red Grouse

THE RED grouse is probably the only truly resident bird on the Long Mynd. They are wholly dependent on the heather and feed almost exclusively on young heather and bilberry shoots. They are most active in the few hours after dawn especially around Pole Cottage, Shooting Box and Boiling Well. Grouse are about the size of farmyard hens and have a rich red-brown speckled plumage which blends well with the colours of the open moor. They are extremely well camouflaged and lie still if approached whereupon the male may fly off with short whirring wings or glide over the heather making a characteristic cackling call so causing a distraction while the female stays put on her nest or hides in nearby heather. They are on the national amber list (Long Mynd, very high priority).

Grouse are plump and tasty and so have been the most popular game bird in Britain since the mid nineteenth century. Grouse shooting did not become a widespread sport until the advent of the breech-loader gun in 1853 and the coming of the railway. Before 1752, the annual shooting season used to begin on the 1st August, the date being dictated by the end of the bird's breeding season. However, when England changed from using the old Julian calendar to the Gregorian calendar, 11 days had to be added, hence the 12th August. The 'glorious twelfth' was a pivotal date in many a sportsman's diary and Parliament made sure that it

was always in recess in good time for members to make their way to the northern moors. It is not surprising that they are the subject of many paintings by artists such as Archibald Thorburn and Martin Ridley.

The Long Mynd used to be managed for grouse shooting and bags of 100 brace per day were not uncommon around 1900. Numbers of grouse declined steadily during the 20th century and shooting was eventually stopped in 1990. By the year 2000 the number of grouse had decreased to dangerously low numbers and heather management was pointless as the sheep fed preferentially in any burnt areas and prevented any regrowth of the heather. Now with a significant reduction in sheep numbers and active heather management, grouse numbers have slowly improved to 60–63 pairs in 2012.

In order to maintain a good grouse population, the heather must not get too woody or so dense that the birds cannot move about. For these reasons, the National Trust burns or cuts sections of heather in rotation so that there is always some new heather growth for the grouse. The burns are kept small and narrow (less than 30 m wide) because the females and chicks like to remain within 15 m of tall heather for cover whilst they are feeding on the young shoots.

Red grouse chick.

© Hilary Chambers

© Hilary Chambers

Red Grouse.

© Anne Burgess

Red grouse droppings are often seen in heaps like this and likened to cigarette butts.

Snipe

S NIPE ARE birds of the mires and ponds of the Long Mynd plateau. They are medium sized wading birds, about the size of a blackbird, which are a well-camouflaged mottled brown colour. Their most characteristic feature is their huge straight 7–8 cm beak, the sensitive tip of which they use to probe the soft ground for worms, snails, insects and larvae. Their eyes are set far back on its head so that they can still see when the beak is plunged full length into mud. When flushed, they fly off with a zig-zag flight. Snipe numbers have declined rapidly in recent years and there are now only one or two pairs breeding on the Long Mynd. They are on the national amber list (Long Mynd, very high priority).

Snipe are the most secretive of all the birds on the Long Mynd although there are hundreds of them from October until the first frosts of the winter as they pass through on their migration from Scandinavia and Russia. They then disappear south or to the coast in freezing weather. They are only regularly found close to the boggy area around Wildmoor Pool and the stream that runs into it but are more likely to be heard than seen. They make a characteristic vibrato 'drumming' noise early and late in the day, a sound which carries over a long distance. It is thought that the sound arises from vibrations in their outer tail feathers which flap like a flag when the male dives.

In Old English, the word snipe was originally *snite* meaning a long, thin object. The modern verb 'to snipe' meaning to shoot at a single person or to single out a person for criticism appears to come directly from the shape of the bird's beak.

Snipe have long been prized by wildfowlers and, along with woodcock, are the only waders that may legally be killed and sold. Mrs Beaton, in her recipe for dressed snipe, writes 'they should be sent to the table very hot or they will not be worth eating'.

Curlew

THE HAUNTING call of the curlew is one of the most evocative sounds of the spring and summer moorland where the melancholy sound drifts across the heather. The call of a curlew in such a place is probably the most wonderful wild sound in Britain. The best time to see and hear them is during their display flights in the spring and up to mid June.

Unfortunately curlew numbers have decreased markedly in recent years due to predation by crows and by modern farming methods such as the early cutting of grass for silage. They are down to just two or three pairs on the Long Mynd and are on the national amber list (Long Mynd, high priority).

The curlew is Britain's largest wader, almost the size of a herring gull, and is instantly recognised by its long, down-curved thin bill, brown upper parts and long legs. Robert Burns is said to have called them 'lang, leggity beasties'. Its bill has a flexible tip which is sensitive to movement allowing the curlew to detect and catch prey up to 15 cm below the surface of soft ground or mud.

Curlews have been popular birds for the table over many centuries. A list of permitted selling prices issued by order of Edward I in 1275 stated that it should be 3d. By 1384, the price had risen to 6d each. At the coronation feast of Henry VI, curlew were on the menu along with plover, larks, swan, heron, crane and bittern.

Cuckoo

THERE IS A good chance of hearing a cuckoo calling in April or May, especially around New Pool Reservoir and in The Batch. Juvenile cuckoos are seen on the Long Mynd and it is assumed that eggs have been laid in meadow pipit's nests since they are the favoured foster parent. Cuckoos are one of the few British birds that everyone can identify by call alone. Only the male bird makes the familiar far-carrying cry which he uses to attract a mate from vast distances; the female makes a soft bubbling sound like water being poured from a bottle. Cuckoos are on the national amber list.

Cuckoos are a harbinger of spring and tradirionally the subject of letters to *The Times*. They are the only British bird which lays its eggs in other bird's nests, laying one in each of a dozen or more suitable nests, typically meadow pipit, dunnock, reed warbler or pied wagtail. The hen cuckoo has the ability to lay eggs to match the colour of her host's eggs, albeit bigger. As the chick hatches along with the chicks of their host, the strapping cuckoo chick evicts the other chicks and any eggs of its host by hoisting them onto its back and tipping them over the edge of the nest. As it grows, its voracious appetite demands ever more food from the frantic foster parents trying to satisfy their strange chick (see photograph opposite). Once it fledges, the young cuckoo goes on its way, alone, to Africa without any assistance, in fact, it never knowingly sees its real parents.

Cuckoos are about the size of kestrels and often are mistaken for sparrowhawks because of their pointed wings and similar colouring. They have dark grey backs and a barred front. They perch in trees in a prominent position looking for large caterpillars, including the hairy ones which other birds reject. The name came with the Normans from the Old French *cucu*. The cuckoo has been associated with many folk tales and traditions. For example, there was a widespread belief that hearing a cuckoo after midsummer portends illness or death.

Calling someone a cuckoo has implied that they were stupid and cloud-cuckoo land is a nineteenth century allusion to fantasy. The notion that the cuckoo spent its day in song while other birds reared their young gives rise to the word cuckold. It was the cuckold, like the meadow pipit who kept up the home while the cuckoo lover romped with his wife. There was certainly the suggestion that the husband must have been pretty dim-witted to have been hoodwinked in the first place:

> *The cuckoo then on every tree*
> *Mocks married men, for thus sings he*
> *'Cuckoo'.*

Satellite tracking of a cuckoo has provided the first information about where cuckoos go after they leave Britain. A male, was ringed in Norfolk in May 2011. He left England at the end of June after spending only about six weeks to find a mate and establish a territory. He was tracked to Auvergne, France, then spent 3 weeks in Italy leaving on 21st July He then spent the next eight months in Chad, Nigeria, Central African Republic, Congo, Ghana and Ivory Coast. On 1st April 2012, he crossed the Sahara via Mali and Algeria to southern Spain where he is feared to have died on 6th April, possibly due to very bad weather. In his travels he achieved speeds of 62 mph and covered a huge range of west and central Africa.

© Michael Callan/FLPA

The meadow pipit continues to feed the baby cuckoo through to maturity.

Teal

TEALS ARE the smallest British duck. The drake has a chestnut coloured head with broad green eye stripe, a finely speckled cream chest, grey flanks and a black edged yellow tail whilst the females are mottled brown. Both show bright green wing patches (speculum) in flight.

© Mark Robinson

They are dabbling ducks which are sometimes seen during the winter months on those Long Mynd pools where there is plenty of emergent vegetation such as Wildmoor pool. They nest in dense vegetation and so are rarely seen during the breeding season. They are on the national amber list (Long Mynd, very high priority) and have not bred here in recent years.

The collective name, a spring of teal, is an appropriate description of their readiness to take to flight almost vertically from the water and wheel and turn in tight small flocks.

Jay

JAYS ARE the most colourful members of the crow family and are shy woodland birds, rarely moving far from cover. Their screaming call is usually given when flying between the trees where its distinctive flash of blue on the wing and white on the rump may be seen. They are common in mature deciduous woods on the edge of the Long Mynd, such as Rectory Wood. Jays particularly like oak trees in the autumn when there are plenty of acorns; they have been known to bury up to five thousand for retrieving later in the winter. Some authorities say that jays have played a part in the spreading of oak forests through this habit.

Ring Ouzel

RING OUZELS are mountain and moorland blackbirds and are rarely seen in other habitats. They winter in southern Spain and the Atlas Mountains of Morocco and are often seen on spring passage on the Long Mynd. Unfortunately the population is declining all over Britain and the local decline has been catastrophic. The last time they bred on the Long Mynd was in 2003. They are on the national red list (Long Mynd, very high priority).

Male ring ouzels are similar to common blackbirds in shape and size but they appear a bit more grey and have a prominent white throat and band across the breast which gives them their name. Ring ouzels usually nest on steep hillsides, broken by crags and scree. Nests are built under heather bushes and they feed on insects and worms in short grass. In the past, most of the records have come from the valleys on the eastern side of the Long Mynd. They are very elusive, the males sing only sporadically but when they nested here a pair would be been seen feeding together, either prior to egg laying at the end of April, or later in the season in the period between fledging the first brood and laying the next clutch.

Ouzel is the oldest name of the blackbird and comes from Old English. The name was only changed to blackbird in the seventeenth century.

Tawny Owl

OWLS ARE unmistakable birds and the tawny and barn owl are easily recognisable. Whilst the barn owl is a bird of the meadows and farms, the tawny owl is a bird of the woods and woodland edges. On the Long Mynd, tawny owls are common in the surrounding woods. This owl became officially known as the tawny owl in the eighteenth century rather than the older name brown owl or grey owl. In Shropshire, it was given the name 'billy hooter'.

Owls are characterised by their large black eyes with pupils twice as large as those of a human which gives them good light gathering ability and helps their night vision. Perhaps more important is their acute hearing that can pick up high frequency sounds such as the rustling of dried leaves made by field mice, shrews, earth worms, frogs and young rabbits. Their hearing is aided by having one ear higher up the head than the other in order to locate the source of sounds. They also have very soft feathers on the leading edges of their wings which allows them to glide silently towards their prey.

The familiar *tu whit, tu whoo* call is heard when a pair are calling to each other at dusk, the male making the hooting *tu whoo* while the female makes a sharp *tu whit* call. The *whoo* part is made mostly during the breeding season. In the autumn, the call is heard when they are fighting over territorial rights.

> *'Tis the middle of night by the castle clock*
> *And the owls have awakened the crowing cock;*
> *Tu-whit!- Tu-whoo!*
> Samuel Taylor Coleridge

Many of the beliefs and superstitions accorded to tawny owls in Britain probably originated with other owl species and are attributed to wisdom, such as the wise old owl image in the *Winnie the Pooh* stories of A A Milne. It has given its name to the Brown Owls who lead the Brownies section of Girlguiding and who are supposed to give wise council to the young girls.

In English folklore, a dead owl served many purposes including mixing some of its flesh with boar's grease as an ointment to ease the pain of gout, and owl broth was once used to feed children to avoid whooping cough. The custom of nailing an owl to a barn door to ward off evil and lightning persisted into the 19th century.

Shakespeare alluded to these traditions in *Macbeth's* witches' brew which contained wing of owl:

> *Eye of newt, and toe of frog,*
> *Wool of bat, and tongue of dog,*
> *Adder's fork, and blind-worm's sting,*
> *Lizard's leg, and howlet's wing,*
> *For a charm of powerful trouble,*
> *Like a hell-broth boil and bubble.*

The tawny owl's range of bizarre screeches, hisses, wails and moans gives them the association with malevolence and death. These sounds are still used as a device to indicate mystery, darkness, suspense and the presence of evil in, for example, films.

Short-eared Owl

© Ian Paterson

THE 'EARS' of the short-eared owl are short tufts of feathers which can barely be seen, in contrast to those on the long-eared owl. The owl's main characteristic feature is the very obvious barred brown and white plumage. Short-eared owls are winter visitors to the Long Mynd and are active during the daytime. They are the same size as the tawny owl but have longer wings and an irregular flight. They feed on a wide variety of rodents and other small animals and are birds of the open country and moorland. Short-eared owls are on the national amber list.

Hobby

THE POPULATION of hobbies in Britain is expanding rapidly northwards from the lowland heath of southern England and they have bred for a number of years in Shropshire. They are a summer visitor and are regularly seen hawking large insects high above the Long Mynd plateau. They can look like a large swift with their long scythe-shaped wings as they hunt for large flying insects high in the sky in the early morning and at dusk. They will also take small birds, especially those like swallows and swifts that also hunt insects.

Hobbies are slightly smaller than kestrels and twice the size of swifts. They have a similar coloration to that of the peregrine falcon. They get their name from the French *hobereau* derived from the Old French *hober*, meaning 'to stir', an allusion to its method of suddenly charging into a flock of swallows or martins.

© Stéphane Aubry

Woodpeckers

ALL WOODPECKERS have a stout, relatively long, sharply pointed chisel bill and robust body designed for chiselling into tree trunks and branches for wood-boring insects and for excavating nest holes. Woodpecker feet are well adapted to climbing trees, with two toes pointing forward and two back (one of which can also be bent sideways to improve grip) and a stiff tail to act as a rigid strut when hammering at a tree. Their sensitive tongue is extremely long with sticky saliva at its tip which is used for extracting insects from holes. One has only to imagine how much effort making such holes would require with a hammer and chisel and you have some sense of the woodpecker's enormous strength.

Great Spotted Woodpecker

© Hilary Chambers

THE GREAT spotted woodpecker is about the size of a blackbird; its colour is a striking black and white with a bright red patch at the back of its head and red under its tail. It has a very distinctive bouncing flight and spends most of its time clinging to tree trunks and branches, often trying to hide on the side away from the observer. They are restricted to the mature woodlands on the edge of the Long Mynd as well as scattered trees on the hillsides and in gardens.

Its presence is often announced by its loud *kik* call or by a distant and distinctive 'drumming' noise, particularly in the spring as a territorial display. The sound is not caused by the woodpecker's attempts to excavate a hole or search for grubs but rather made at the correct frequency of knocks (10–40 strikes per second) to make the timber resonate. It is actually a territorial display carried out by the male to attract a mate. To avoid damage to the head there is shock-absorbent tissue at the base of the skull.

Green Woodpecker

THE GREEN woodpecker is the largest of the three woodpeckers that breed in Britain. They are unmistakable birds with olive-green backs, a paler belly, red head and throat, black patch over its eyes and cheeks and a yellow rump They are large birds, about the size of a jackdaw and are regularly seen in the lower reaches of Long Mynd valleys where there are large mature deciduous trees and in the neighbouring fields and gardens.

Green woodpeckers spend most of their time feeding on ants on the ground where there is short grass. This is aided by their tongue which is armed with barbs at the end. It is so long (10 cm) that it has to be curled round inside its skull. It will dismantle anthills and is unperturbed by the swarming ants. Green woodpeckers differ from most other woodpeckers in having a soft bill and so do not hammer.

The green woodpecker has an undulating flight and a loud, laughing call which gives rise to its common name 'yaffle'. It is on the national amber list.

The long tongue of a woodpecker can be extended to 10 cm beyond the bill and is anchored near to the right nostril.

Breeding Territories

Most species of birds are dependent on particular niche and vegetation types, and some are restricted to either the plateau or the valley sides. The breeding territory of any bird has four fundamental requirements:

Cover to hide the nest and to keep eggs and nestlings safe from predators.
Cover for the adults to keep them safe from predators while resting and roosting.
A song post or display area for males to proclaim territory and attract a mate.
Areas to gather food.

All these different territory requirements must be located within the small area of each territory. Many priority species of bird are dependent on wetlands (pools and flushes), bracken, short grass, trees and/or habitat variety. Examples relevant to birds on the Long Mynd are shown below.

Species dependent on wetland:
Teal require pools with emergent vegetation to feed and hide ducklings.
Snipe require soft wet ground.
Reed buntings require acid and wet flush for food.

Species dependent on bracken:
Tree pipits and redstarts feed on the ground as well as in trees.
Whinchats are virtually restricted to bracken habitats on hillsides and by springs or pools.

Species dependent on short grass:
Curlew require short grass for feeding and for somewhere to land at the end of their display flight.
Skylarks require short grass for feeding. In longer grass they are replaced by meadow pipit.
Redstarts feed on the short grass under the scattered trees.
Stonechats feed on areas of short vegetation and grass.
Wheatears are restricted to areas of very short grass and badly eroded hillside. Rabbit holes provide the nest sites.
Ring ouzels require areas of short grass for feeding.

Species dependent on a combination of habitats:
Stonechats nest near the boundary of different vegetation types and feeds in each.
Whinchats nest near bracken and water.

Species dependent on trees:
Buzzards build their nest in trees.
Tree pipits display and feed in trees.
Grey wagtails get supplementary food from trees.
Redstarts nest in holes in trees and feed in the foliage.
Yellowhammers sings from trees and feed in the foliage.

Species indirectly dependent on trees:
Kestrels and merlins lay eggs in old crow's nests.

Predation of ground nesting birds is a particular cause for concern and ring ouzel, teal, snipe and curlew have all suffered a big decline directly as a result of attacks on their nests and young. Foxes and crows are believed to be the main culprits but their elimination is almost impossible because as soon as any are removed, others would come in from the nearby countryside to fill any vacuum created here.

Mammals

OR THE daytime walker, the Long Mynd may seem almost devoid of mammals. In fact, the small ones are hidden by the bracken and heather and are very shy, whilst the larger ones are mainly nocturnal. Foxes, badgers and bats are common all over the plateau as well as in the peripheral woods and are readily seen at dusk. Most of the other species found on or around the Long Mynd require some effort to see them and a degree of luck. To get a real idea of the diversity of wildlife on the Long Mynd you need to have the skills of a good detective.

However, all animals leave signs of their presence and the ability to recognise these signs adds a whole new dimension to walking. Success in seeing mammals depends to some extent on the time of day and the season. The hours around dawn and dusk are always a good time since mammals are at their most active searching for food. Learning to recognise animal tracks and footprints in soft ground and snow, and their paths through grass and undergrowth, can be rewarding. Feeding signs to look out for are gnawing marks on trees and saplings, nut shells and conifer cones, and the remains of feathers and carcasses. It helps also to be an expert on animal droppings!

The Batch

© Lucas Littlewood

Otter eating a chick.

Otter

OTTERS, THOUGH rarely seen, are well established in the larger rivers of South Shropshire and they readily explore further afield to the smaller streams. Evidence for their presence may only be by their footprints or black greasy looking spraints (faeces) left on prominent rocks. Individual otters have been seen in the New Pool Hollow reservoir and in other valleys on both sides of the Long Mynd. They have even been known to take fish from garden ponds in Church Stretton.

The population of otters had been decimated in the 1950s and 1960s by the combined effects of organochlorine pesticides, habitat destruction by the removal of stream-side vegetation, the draining of wetlands, and pollution in general. Fortunately, significant improvement to the purity of rivers has allowed them to extend their range slowly; their presence in a river is a sensitive measure of its purity.

© Robert Raynor

Otters charm people with their lovable faces and playful behaviour. For many, their first encounter is through the story of Gavin Maxwell's *Ring of Bright Water* or Henry Williamson's sad tale of *Tarka the Otter* in which Tarka is eventually hunted and killed by hounds. The barbaric hunting of otters with dogs continued through to 1978 when it became illegal.

Many a supposed sighting of the Loch Ness Monster may be attributed to the otter's habit of several sometimes swimming in line astern with only the head of the lead otter above the water. All that can be seen from afar is a head and a series of humps!

Otter spraints are typically found on rocks in streams. Note the bits of fish bone and scales in the faeces.

Polecat

POLECATS are more likely to be seen dead on a road than alive. The Marches and the West Midlands are now a stronghold for this animal in England and they probably exist on the farmland around the Long Mynd. Polecats are nocturnal animals with a well-developed fear of man. They are ferocious killers and will attack anything up to the size of a rabbit. They are about 55 cm long, of which about 15 cm is tail.

Polecats have beautiful markings on their face and body, varying from black, brown, ginger, cream and white. Their domesticated version, the ferret, is similar though often it is a cream or brown colour and has been used since Roman times for hunting rabbits. When ferrets escape they can breed with polecats to form polecat-ferret hybrids and many of the animals on the fringes of the polecat's range may be hybrids. These hybrids often die because they are not fierce enough.

Polecats used to be called 'foulmart' meaning 'foul marten' an allusion to the disgusting smell which they exude from their anal glands. Their Latin name *putorius* is very appropriate!

© Peter Trimming

Stoat

FOR MANY people, their encounters with a live stoat are limited to a sleek, sinuous, brown animal on busy legs dashing across the road in front of their car. Like all their mustelid cousins, mink, weasels and polecats, they rightly deserve their reputation for being aggressive and vicious out of all proportion to their size. Their teeth are notoriously sharp and are used to ruthlessly kill their prey, often rabbits, water voles and rats, with a bite to the back of their neck. Stoats are present on and around the Long Mynd living in rock crevasses and old rabbit holes. One was seen carrying a live rabbit to the water's edge of the New Pool Hollow reservoir and pushing it below the water to drown it.

Stoats are about 35 cm long from head to tail. Their fur is a rich chocolate brown above and white below and always have a characteristic black tip to their tail. In winter, stoats from Scotland and the northern part of England turn white whilst keeping their black tip to the tail. The colour change is quite rapid and

Juvenile stoat.

depends partly on hereditary and partly controlled by temperature. Their new white coat grows beneath the old one and becomes apparent when the old coat is shed.

Their white pelts are called ermine and form part of the prized regalia of royalty, peers of the realm and certain other personages as decreed by Henry IV. The black spots on the robes are the tips of the ermine's tails.

Stoats appear in children's literature; the stoat, Wild Wooders, is the ruffian in Kenneth Grahame's *Wind in the Willows*.

Weasel

WEASELS are smaller than stoats, being about 25 cm from head to tail. They lack the black tip to the tail but otherwise may easily be confused with a stoat. Their prey is smaller animals, typically young rabbits, mice and voles but size for size they are probably more aggressive than stoats. They do not turn white in the winter like stoats.

Weasel.

Badger

BADGERS are common on and around the Long Mynd with large family groups living in an extensive system of underground tunnels called setts, especially in the deciduous woods on the lower slopes. Some setts have been known to be over a century old. Small setts used by solitary or pairs of badgers may appear anywhere on the hillsides. Being nocturnal animals, they are rarely seen during the day. Badgers are more likely to be seen dead for they are the frequent victim of collisions with cars on the road. If they survive cars, they can live for up to fourteen years.

Badgers are big animals with a fully grown male growing to a metre long. When hunting at night they snuffle around amongst the leaf litter for earthworms which is their preferred diet but they readily eat mice, slugs, hedgehogs, apples and carrion. They are particularly fond of wasps' and bees' nests which they dig up principally for the larvae. They will also take bird chicks especially in dry weather when worms are hard to find.

They are popular animals, perhaps because of their colouration and shuffling behaviour. In children's stories such as *Wind in the Willows* and in the *Rupert Bear* annuals they are depicted as trustworthy, wise, kind and genial. The old Celtic name for them is *broc* which has given its name to local villages and places like Brockton and Brockhurst.

The badger's fur has been sought for use in fine artist's brushes and shaving brushes. Badger pelts are used to make the finest sporrans and have also been used by native Americans for trim to their garments.

Badgers have always been persecuted and badger baiting has been a rural pastime for centuries. It was outlawed as long ago as 1835 but the practice continued under various guises despite Acts of Parliament. A formidable adversary for any dog, the badger was a sought-after participant for the fighting pit. When cornered it possesses impressive courage and with its extremely powerful claws and bite it is more than capable of injuring a dog. The dog most used for hunting badgers has been the dachshund. It was bred in Germany to hunt badgers and rabbits to follow them to ground inside the burrows where they could fight the prey to the death. *Dachs* is the German word for badger.

A new controversy has arisen with the trials being carried out to determine the association between tuberculosis in cattle and badgers. Whilst there is a proven link, it is unclear what the method of transmission is, though infected badgers under stress urinating on pasture land are a contributory factor. The law has now been changed to allow badgers in certain areas to be legally killed. There is no evidence for tuberculosis in badgers in Shropshire.

Brown Hare

Hares are much bigger than rabbits and differ particularly in their habits. They are solitary, not colonial and do not burrow, preferring to rest in a depression in long grass, called a form. They rely on their acute senses and their ability to run very fast, up to 70 km/h. The brown hare was probably introduced during the Iron Age from Scandinavia. They occur on the farmland surrounding the Long Mynd and have been seen on the hill amongst the heather.

A female can rear three or four litters a year, each of two to four young. The young, known as leverets, are born fully furred with their eyes open and are left by the female in forms a few metres from their birth place. Once a day for the first four weeks of their lives, the leverets gather at sunset to be fed by the female, but otherwise they receive no parental care. This avoids attracting predators to the young at a stage when they are most vulnerable. Foxes are important predators of young hares and where foxes are common there are likely to be fewer hares.

The so-called March hare madness is part of their breeding behaviour. Rapid chases may involve a dominant male driving a rival away from a female he is guarding. Two hares may rear up on their ungainly long hind legs and appear to be boxing with their paws. It is usually a rebuff given by a female to an over-amorous male and may occur at any time in the long breeding season but is most visible in March when there are lighter evenings and the vegetation is still low. This apparent grotesque behaviour gives rise to hares being thought of as being stupid or mad.

Lewis Carroll depicted this in *Alice's Adventures in Wonderland* in which he wrote:

> *The Hatter shook his head mournfully. 'Not I!' he replied. 'We quarrelled last March - just before he went mad, you know', pointing with his teaspoon at the March Hare.*

Alice, the March Hare and the Mad Hatter.

Fox

THE FOX IS the most widespread carnivore in the world and inevitably the most successful. About the same size as a typical dog, it is characterised by its rich red-brown coloration, pointed muzzle, black-tipped erect ears and very bushy tail. Foxes are more often heard than seen. The vixen in the mating season, from January onwards, can emit an unearthly scream which is unbelievably similar to the human voice.

Foxes are common on and around the Long Mynd. They have a wide and varied diet which may consist of field voles, rabbits, earthworms, beetles, small birds, blackberries and carrion. Following the myxomatosis epidemic among rabbits in the 1950s and the collapse of the rabbit population, the fox became urbanised, travelling into towns at night to scavenge for food.

Foxes are one of the few animals that humans can detect immediately from their 'foxy' or sour, sharp scent which results from urine marking. Their scats are territorial markers and they deposit them in prominent locations such as grass tussocks.

Foxes have always been labelled as sly, wily and cunning, although children's stories do not necessarily depict them as evil in the same way as the wolf. Foxes are considered as rogues, a bit caddish and occasionally, as in A A Milne's *Three Little Foxes,*

'who didn't wear stockings and didn't wear sockses'

almost lovable. The most successful modern literary fox is Roald Dahl's *Fantastic Mr Fox* which tells the story of a fox that consistently gained the better of the rich and nasty farmers Boggis, Bunce and Bean.

To the farmer and smallholder, foxes are pests and considered a threat to their livestock, especially poultry and lambs. They have always been hunted by one means or another and it was inevitable that fox hunting grew into a sport and the basis for a significant rural industry. Everyone knows the song of the huntsman John Peel;

© Peter Trimming

D'ye ken John Peel with his coat so gay?
D'ye ken John Peel at the break o' day?
D'ye ken John Peel when he's far, far a-way.
With his hounds and his horn in the morning?

For the sound of his horn brought me from my bed,
And the cry of his hounds which he oft time led,
Peel's 'View, Halloo!' could awaken the dead,
Or the fox from his lair in the morning.
[John Woodcock Graves, 1795–1886]

Inevitably, the fox gave its name to pubs though there are none in the immediate vicinity. Fox is also a common surname originally adopted by people with some fox-like characteristics.

Fox cubs.

Mink

THE AMERICAN mink is not a native species and was introduced in 1929, destined to become breeding stock in commercial fur farms to provide the ultimate status symbol of fashion. Mink soon escaped and together with those deliberately released by misguided 'animal rights' groups have become widespread throughout Britain. They can be mistaken for an otter but are much smaller, being half the length, about the size of a ferret. They now breed in the wild with disastrous consequences for their prey which, besides rabbits, consists of ground-nesting birds and their eggs (especially moorhens and coots), poultry, fish and water voles.

They have been recorded along the margins of the Long Mynd but their population seems to be declining, possibly as a result of increasing numbers of otters who see them as an alien competitor to be killed at every opportunity.

The word mink comes from the Swedish *menk* meaning 'a stinking animal from Finland'.

Water Shrew

WATER SHREWS are the largest of the five species of shrews in Britain and like all shrews leads a hectic life, busy by day and night on the look-out for food. The animal is very small so it quickly burns up its energy reserves and if it did not feed continuously, it would die within a few hours. They are present in many of the valley streams on the edge of the Long Mynd.

Water shrews live close to fresh water, hunting aquatic insects, snails, molluscs and small amphibians (especially newts) and other prey in the water and nearby. They can even swim underwater to catch caddisfly and mayfly larvae. Although they do not have webbed feet, a fringe of stiffer hairs on their back feet and hairs on their tail aid swimming. Their fur traps bubbles of air when in the water which greatly aids their buoyancy.

Water shrews usually lives alone and each one occupies a territory which it fiercely defends from other shrews. Fighting is common and shrill squeals can sometimes be heard when a territorial dispute takes place. Each shrew digs a shallow burrow system, sometimes in a bank, with a tunnel leading to a nest chamber which is lined with a ball of grass, roots and moss. The burrow system may have an underwater entrance as well.

Like many shrews, the water shrew has venomous saliva making it one of the few venomous mammals, although it is not able to puncture the skin of large animals such as humans. Its mouth is full of sharp, pointed teeth which allow it to hang on to prey securely as it chews. It eats roughly its own body weight in food each day.

The water shrew does not like being in the water for long and often comes ashore to dry itself. It squeezes along the narrow passageways of its tunnel to get rid of the water from its fur and then grooms itself thoroughly.

The water shrew is sometimes regarded as a pest because it eats the spawn of valuable fish stocks. Normally though, they are shy and secretive and are rarely seen and difficult to spot. If you are walking quietly along the bank of a slow-moving, clear, shallow stream or in a watercress field, you may hear its shrill squeaks amongst the vegetation and even see the shrew's tiny footprints in the mud along a river bank.

Wood Mouse

THE MOUSE is probably the best known of all animals, instantly recognisable and one that is featured in countless books and stories generally in sympathetic portrayals. Of the three native 'outdoor' mice, the harvest mouse, yellow-necked mouse and the brown wood mouse, the latter is by far the most abundant, though the yellow-necked mouse also has a stronghold in this area. The 'indoor' mouse, the grey house mouse, along with the brown and black rat have been introduced to Britain. Mice differ from voles by having a pointed face and a relatively long tail.

The wood mouse is the mouse of grassland, gardens and hedges and is common around the perimeter of the Long Mynd and has also been seen at Pole Cottage.

They are difficult to approach closely because of their very good eyesight, acute hearing and sensitivity to vibration. They breed at a phenomenal rate and as such provide the staple diet of many predators such as owls and foxes. The wood mouse is the mouse a cat proudly brings into one's house.

It is the wood mouse, not the house mouse, that is the inspiration for Beatrix Potter's 'Appley Dapply'

> Appley Dapply, a little brown mouse,
> Goes to the cupboard in somebody's house.
> In somebody's cupboard there's everything nice,
> Cake, cheese, jam, biscuits all charming for mice!
> Appley Dapply has little sharp eyes,
> And Appley Dapply is so fond of pies!

© Hilary Chambers

Wood mice have noticeably large ears. They are usually the culprit when stores of fruit or seeds are eaten in garden sheds.

© Peter Trimming

© Robert Raynor

© Nick Picozzii

Field Vole

F IELD VOLES and their close relative the bank vole are together the most abundant of all British mammals and the favourite food of owls. The field vole is common around the perimeter of the Long Mynd and has also been seen at Pole Cottage. They have short, stubby faces and short tails. Voles differ from mice in being strictly vegetarian, eating the grass in which they live and make their runs. Their name comes from the Norwegian *vollmus* meaning field mouse.

Left: Fresh field vole faeces (about 6 mm long) and (above) its run.

Bats

© Graeme Smith

Pipistrelle bat.

BATS ARE the only warm-blooded mammals to have successfully evolved to take to the air by greatly extending their finger bones to support thin membranes which allow them to fly. Although they have functional eyes, they are not 'as blind as a bat' and have evolved highly sensitive ultrasonic echo-location ears which allow them to search for moths and other insects at night. Bats as a group are evolutionarily very successful animals; almost a quarter of all species of mammals are bats.

Bats are important members of the woodland community, foraging in or near trees and roosting in cracks, holes, and crevices in the bark of trees. Female bats try to form huge nursery colonies containing several hundred adults and young, males being excluded. Bats have a high metabolic rate that demands a huge amount of food; a single bat may eat up to seventy moths each night. In the winter when their food supply disappears they hibernate, not in church belfries which are too cold and draughty, but in hollow trees, old buildings or in house attics.

The bat's a radar guided gent
For night time's flying he is meant
The art is not to snag your hair
(Unless you're hiding insects there).

Ogden Nash

Ten bat species are regularly seen foraging in or near woods and old buildings around the perimeter of the Long Mynd. In particular, the brown long-eared, common pipistrelle, soprano pipistrelle, noctule, lesser horseshoe and whiskered bat. Pipistrelle and brown long-eared bats are the commonest species and most likely to be seen in the evening hunting for moths and other flying insects. Lesser horseshoe bats have been seen at the entrance to the New Pool Hollow reservoir tunnel.

Bats have a bad reputation. They have ugly faces, disproportionately long ears, strange looking wing-like membranes and are generally ungainly creatures. To crown it all, some tropical bats are blood-drinkers. Nevertheless, they are protected by law and it is illegal to disturb a roost.

Bat identification is usually done by an electronic 'bat detector' gadget that alters the frequency (note) of the bat's emitted ultrasonic 'click' by scaling the frequency down into the human hearing range. Thus a pipistrelle emits ultrasonic sound in the range of 53 to 91 kHz, but when electronically reduced by a factor of 16, the new frequency range is 3.3 to 5.7 kHz, easily within our hearing range. Sonograms can now be recorded and reproduced afterwards as frequency-time graphs which are characteristic of each species.

The name 'bat' comes from the Middle English *bakke*. The Germans call it *fledermaus*, flying mouse, made familiar from the opera of that name.

© Hugh Clark, Bat Conservation Trust

Pipistrelle bat

Mole

MOLES ARE widespread in the fields around the Long Mynd, especially in the enclosed fields in The Batch at All Stretton and on the summit in the improved grassland around old sheep feeding sites. Moles are common in grassy areas wherever the soil is soft enough for tunnelling and earthworms are plentiful.

They are well adapted to life underground and it is rare for one to be seen. They would, however, be immediately recognised by their powerful spade-like forefeet, short cylindrical body, pointed pink nose and short velvety fur.

Each mole has its own burrow system, a network of firm-walled tunnels with sleeping chambers lined with grass, moss and leaves. The tunnels are about 5 cm wide, 4 cm high and may be over 70 metres long; they vary in depth from just beneath the surface to about 70 cm below ground. When tunnelling, a mole uses one front foot to push soil upwards into a molehill (or tump) while it braces the other and the hind feet firmly against the tunnel walls. It can excavate up to 20 m of tunnel in a day.

> *Diggory Diggory Delvet!*
> *A little old man in black velvet;*
> *He digs and he delves -*
> *You can see for yourselves*
> *The mounds dug by Diggory Delvet.*
> [Traditional nursery rhyme]

The territories of several moles may overlap but the residents avoid each other if they can except in the breeding season. A mole can run backwards through tunnels; its velvety fur lies backwards or forwards so that it does not become stuck against the tunnel walls when squeezing through them.

A mole's diet primarily consists of earthworms and other small invertebrates found in the soil. The mole runs are in reality worm traps, the mole sensing when a worm falls into the tunnel and quickly runs along to kill and eat it. Because their saliva contains a toxin that can paralyse earthworms, moles are able to store their still living prey for later consumption. They construct special underground larders for just this purpose which have been known to hold over a thousand earthworms in them. Before eating earthworms, moles pull them between their squeezed paws to force the collected earth and dirt out of the worm's gut.

Moles are sometimes seen above ground, emerging mainly at night but they are still vulnerable to predators, especially owls. They come to the surface to collect nesting material and to look for food when the soil is dry. Young moles come to the surface and travel overland to look for new homes when they leave their mother's burrow. It is during this venture above ground that tawny owls can take up to 45% of them.

Although moles are loathed by gardeners and farmers, they are adored by children who love the likes of Mole in Kenneth Grahame's *The Wind in the Willows*.

Carding Mill Valley.

Reptiles and Amphibians

Michael Dibb

Northeastwildlife.co.uk

Grass snake and (inset) egg shells after hatching.

REPTILES AND amphibians are cold-blooded animals which hibernate in Britain, only coming out on a sunny day to bask in a sheltered gap in the vegetation. At first sight, the Long Mynd should be an ideal site for adders with plenty of dry heather and bracken growing on warm sunny hillsides on which to bask. Surprisingly, there have been no sightings of adders. It could be that excessive burning of heather and bracken in the past when the Long Mynd was managed as a grouse moor has contributed to their demise.

Grass Snake

Grass snakes are not found on the Long Mynd but are seen on the margins of the hill where they are associated with damp grassland and pools. They hibernate in garden compost heaps and farm middens in which they also lay their eggs. Grass snakes are excellent swimmers and are rarely seen far from places where their favourite prey of frogs, newts and toads occur.

Common Lizard

Common lizards are seen occasionally, especially in April and September, in Carding Mill Valley, Haddon Hill, Townbrook Valley and near Pole Cottage. If you hear a rustle in the grass or in the litter under bracken or heather plants, then it is likely to be caused by a rapidly disappearing lizard. They feed on small invertebrates, especially spiders which they actively hunt as soon as their body temperature is high enough. Lizards hibernate over winter in crevasses under rocks or in holes.

Their official name, viviparous lizard, alludes to their ability to give birth to live young rather than lay eggs like most other reptiles. The young reptiles still develop within individual egg membranes but inside their mother who acts as a mobile incubator. At birth each egg membrane ruptures, freeing the offspring which are self-reliant and fully independent from then on.

© Stefan Czapski

Common Lizard.

Slow Worm

Slow worms are found on the margins of the Long Mynd where they may be found in dry areas in gardens on the hillside, field banks and at the foot of walls. Whilst their name is descriptive of them, looking worm-like and moving slowly, they are legless lizards. They have a beautiful bronze-coloured iridescent sheen and do not mind being carefully handled. Their favourite food is slugs and as a result are a gardener's best friend.

© Laurent Lebois

Slow worm.

Common Frog

The common frog is by far the commonest amphibian present on the Long Mynd and is the first species to emerge from hibernation in the spring. They lay their frothy mass of spawn (one clump per female) in many of the ponds on the plateau and even in puddles on a track. A typical clump of spawn may contain two thousand eggs and providing it does not dry out or is exposed to severe frost, most of the eggs will hatch out into tadpoles. It is at this stage and later as froglets that they get eaten by hedgehogs, birds and grass snakes. Otters only eat the legs! Their long rear-legs allow them to jump large distances as you soon discover if you try to catch one.

In winter, they hibernate in the sediment at the bottom of ponds where they can survive in a state of torpor for months without directly breathing air because their

© Sylvia Duckworth

highly permeable skin allows oxygen dissolved in the water to be absorbed directly through it.

Common Toad

© Patrick Connolly

Toads CAN readily be distinguished from frogs by having a dry warty skin. Toad spawn is different too, the eggs being laid in long strings which are wrapped around the stems of aquatic vegetation. Common toads are larger than frogs and can be over 10 cm long in old specimens; they can live up to 40 years.

Toads move in a slow ponderous manner and can travel a considerable distance to a particular breeding pond where other toads congregate to mate. They are largely nocturnal and may be found in cool, damp places such as under logs on the margins of the Long Mynd.

The swellings on a toad's skin secrete a poisonous protective substance that most predators find distasteful and this has undoubtedly contributed to their survival. These secretions contain the hallucinogen bufotenine and various glycosides related to the heart stimulant digitalin. Hedgehogs, grass snakes and some birds, particularly buzzards, do not seem to be affected and eat toads with impunity.

Their poisonous skin has contributed to folk medicine and there are many old accounts of toads being implicated in witchcraft. The practice of hanging an object around someone's neck with a view to either curing or preventing something unfortunate from happening was once commonplace and gave rise to toad-doctors. Live toads or parts of toads were commonly placed in bags and suspended on a necklace to this end.

Toads have always been much maligned in literature with the notable exception of Kenneth Grahame's Toad in *The Wind in the Willows*:

> *It's never the wrong time to call on Toad. Early or late, he's always the same fellow. Always good-tempered, always glad to see you, always sorry to see you go ... He is indeed the best of animals ... so simple, so good-natured, and so affectionate. Perhaps he's not very clever - we can't all be geniuses. But he has got some good qualities, has Toady.*

Newts

In general, newts are associated with acid habitats of which the wet areas of the Long Mynd are typical. Of the three species found there, the palmate newt is the most common and breeds in all the pools on the hill. They are the smallest of British newts, reaching a length of 9 cm. The males develop a small crest in the breeding season as well as webbed hind feet which gives them their name. The smooth newt is present in small numbers around the edge of the Long Mynd.

Palmate newts get their name because the males develop webbed feet during the breeding season.

The great crested newt is a much more exotic creature, being up to 16 cm long. In the breeding season the male has a large jagged crest and its underside is bright orange with black spots. The great crested newt has been found recently to breed in a pool on Wildmoor.

In contrast to lizards which can regenerate tails, newts have the remarkable ability to regenerate toes or even complete legs if they are lost or damaged. The name newt comes from the Old English *ewt*. It was probably the palmate newt which reached literary fame as a component of the celebrated witches' brew in Shakespeare's *Macbeth*.

Typical palmate newt habitat.

Butterflies and Moths

COLOUR AND beauty helps their popularity! Most people consider butterflies and, to a lesser extent moths, the most beautiful creatures of the insect kingdom and have attracted attention and interest out of all proportion to their numerical or zoological importance. Of the list of species protected under the Wildlife and Countryside Act (1981), four are butterflies, five are moths and only four are other insects.

The most obvious difference between butterflies and moths is in the feelers, or antennae. Most butterflies have thin slender filamentous antennae which have knobs or clubs at the end. Moths, on the other hand, often have comb-like, feathery or filamentous antennae and are not clubbed. These antennae act as feelers and pick up the presence of airborne chemicals. Moths tend to have stout and hairy or furry-looking bodies while butterflies have slender and smoother abdomens. Moths have larger scales on their wings which makes them look more dense and fluffy. Butterflies, on the other hand, possess fine scales. This difference is possibly due to the need for moths to conserve heat during the cooler nights whereas butterflies need to absorb solar radiation.

Most butterflies rest with their wings held up above their bodies whilst most moths rest with their wings spread out flat.

Common blue butterfly. It is small with a wingspan of only 28 mm.

The order Lepidoptera includes butterflies and moths and is the second largest group in the insect world. The name Lepidoptera means 'scale wings'. If you take a close look at the wings of these insects you will see overlapping scales like shingles on a roof.

Gold spot moth.

Brimstone butterfly.

It is quite fitting that the brimstone butterfly is one of the first species to be described historically since it is generally agreed that the word butterfly is derived from the description of a 'butter-coloured fly' that the male brimstone epitomises. The female is, however, a green colour.

Moths have existed about 100 million years longer than butterflies and get their name from the German *motte*.

> *The little caterpillar creeps*
> *Awhile before in silk it sleeps.*
> *It sleeps awhile before it flies,*
> *And flies awhile before it dies,*
> *And that's the end of three good tries.*
>
> David McCord, *Sing Cocoon*

Small Heath. This is a common but declining grassland butterfly. They spend much of their time weakly fluttering close to the ground, always settling with their wings closed. Wingspan 28-34 mm.

© M Oates

© Robin Webster

The small copper butterfly is common in the Long Mynd valleys. It likes warm dry locations and can often be seen on or near tracks. Common and sheep's sorrel are its favourite food plants.

The purple hairstreak butterfly is common but can be difficult to see because it lives in oak trees. Its upper wings are bluish-purple. It feeds on honeydew and bramble.

© Kev Chapman

© Colin Kinnear

The painted lady butterfly migrates from Southern Europe and North Africa, sometimes in huge numbers.

The orange tip butterfly has quite unmistakable colouring. It lays its eggs on lady's smock and in oak and elm trees.

© Silversypher

© Hilary Chambers

© Evelyn Simak

The green hairstreak butterfly has striking iridescent apple-green underwings.

The small skipper butterfly is common on the Long Mynd, preferring to feed on knapweed and thistles.

The ringlet butterfly prefers moist areas and feeds on a variety of flowers.

© Hilary Chambers

The unique ragged outline distinguishes the comma butterfly from all others and gives it its name. It hibernates over winter and feeds in the autumn on over-ripe fruit.

© Hilary Chambers

© Hilary Chambers

Left: The grayling is a well camouflaged butterfly that likes the arid south facing slopes of the Long Mynd. It lays its eggs in tussocky grass. Fortunately, its numbers are increasing on the Long Mynd but not nationally.
Right: The meadow brown butterfly may be found almost anywhere.

Moths

WHILST MANY moths, especially the night-flying ones, are rather dull and, to the layman, barely distinguishable from one another, some of the day-flying ones are very colourful. In addition, moth caterpillars are often more exotic than those of butterflies. It seems strange that creatures so addicted to a nocturnal lifestyle should so hanker for the brightness of artificial light. The expression 'like moths to a lamp' has become a euphemism for irresistible attraction. The following are just some of the 171 species of moth that have been recorded on the Long Mynd.

© Mike Kirby

The five-spot burnet prefers damp grassland and is seen here feeding on knapweed.

© Hilary Chambers

The mallow moth gets its name from the mallow plant on which it feeds.

© Lairich Rig

© Lairich Rig

Left: The drinker moth and its caterpillar is said to drink dewdrops, hence its name.

Below: The elephant hawk moth lives on honeysuckle whilst the caterpillar prefers rosebay willow herb. The huge caterpillar has two eye spots and looks like an elephant's trunk.

© Eirian Evans

© Evelyn Simak

The fox moth is common on the Long Mynd heather. Its large hairy caterpillar is about 60 mm long and can cause rashes in some people.

The huge adult emperor moth (wingspan 60–85 mm) does not feed but its caterpillar (65 mm long) feeds on heather. The male can be seen flying over the heather searching for females and can detect their pheromones from over a mile away.

The garden tiger moth is boldly coloured to warn predators that its body fluids are poisonous.

The yellow shell moth resembles some shells from which it gets its name.

The huge poplar hawk moth is said to look like a cluster of dead leaves of the main host, the poplar.

Broad-bodied chaser dragonfly.

Dragonflies and Damselflies

DRAGONFLIES and damselflies are amongst the most conspicuous and beautiful invertebrates. They are of similar appearance, dragonflies tend to be larger and rest with their wings apart in contrast to damselflies who usually have them folded back along their body. Dragonflies usually have their eyes touch or nearly touch on top of their head whereas those of damselflies are clearly separated and are often on the side of their head.

Most dragonflies and damselflies prefer water which has soft sediments and, with so many pools, flushes and streams on the Long Mynd, it is not surprising that they are a common insect. Their larvae are carnivorous and are usually the top predator feeding on almost any creature that comes their way.

Like their larvae, adult dragonflies are also superbly adapted predators. They have highly developed compound eyes and wings that beat independently of each other, giving them the ability to fly backwards as well as forwards.

© Hilary Chambers

Common blue damselfly.

© Mick Lobb

This beautiful-demoiselle damselfly lives up to its name showing off its metallic blue body and typical folded wing behaviour when resting.

© M J Richardson

The common hawker is a large and powerful dragonfly which is abundant around the Pole Cottage and Wildmoor ponds where dozens can emerge from a single pond from July to September.

© Dave Green

The male black darter is the only predominantly black dragonfly in Britain. Its habitat is heath land and peat moss and it can be seen perching on vegetation next to a pond. It is very common on the Long Mynd which is one of the major strongholds in Shropshire.

The Golden ringed dragonfly is large, having a length 75–85 mm.

Emperor dragonfly.

Four-spotted chaser dragonfly.

© Hilary Chambers

© Hilary Chambers

Above:
The common darter
dragonfly.

Right:
Southern hawker
dragonfly.

Bees, Wasps and other Invertebrates

Invertebrates are animals without backbones and are essential for the biodiversity of the Long Mynd and can be found in every available niche. They are essential for the pollination of the heather, bilberry, gorse and all the small flowers. In addition, they provide a valuable food source for birds and mammals. The best areas of the Long Mynd for invertebrates is on the valley sides where there is a mosaic of heather, bilberry, gorse, grass and rocky outcrops and also in the area around wet flushes. Below are a few selected examples.

Bees and Wasps

Most of these species on the Long Mynd are solitary with the female solely responsible for making the nest and supplying the food for the developing larvae. In contrast, the social bees and wasps live in large colonies with workers responsible for making the nest and supplying the food. At the end of the breeding season the social structure breaks down and wasps, especially, become annoying around picnic sites where they search for sugary foods.

A pair of social common wasps mating.

Wasps differ from bees in that they feed their young on animal matter including many insect pests whilst bees feed their young on pollen and nectar. Also, unlike bees, wasps are unable to make wax for their nests but instead build them from papery material made from chewing wood fragments. Because of their powerful sting, bees and wasps have few predators; the most notable are green woodpeckers and honey buzzards.

The female tawny mining bee, working alone, excavates a small burrow making small volcano-like mounds of the sandy soil. Beneath are several chambers each lined with a waxy secretion in which she lays her eggs. She then abandons the nest leaving the eggs and larvae to fend for themselves.

In addition to the rich nectar source of bilberry, the bilberry (or mountain) bumblebee also eats clover, bramble, sallow, raspberry and marsh thistle. The rear half of its abdomen is a bright reddish-orange.

Flies

Flies are not the most popular of insects and are far from endearing being considered by most people as pests and carriers of disease. True flies are distinguished from other insects by having only two wings, the hind pair being reduced to vestigial stumps. As Ogden Nash said:

> *God in His wisdom*
> *Made the fly*
> *And then forgot*
> *To tell us why.*

Hover-flies, named because they hover above flowers before landing, are benign except to aphids for which they are a significant predator. They are excellent mimics and are often mistaken for wasps or bees.

The dark giant horse-fly is the largest fly in Europe, measuring 2.5 cm long and is to be found in bogs and moorland on the Long Mynd. It is an intimidating beast characterised by its size and bulging eyes. The female (only) lives by sucking blood. The St Mark's fly, so named because it often makes its first appearance on St Mark's Day, 15 April, is a small black hairy fly that is abundant and often seen flying over the heather in spring and summer. It has unusually long legs and some say that it looks as if it is wearing tiny football boots!

© Silversypher

Hover-fly.

© Silversypher

The dark giant horse-fly.

© Northeastwildlife.co.uk

The St Mark's fly.

Gorse strewn with dew-decked cobwebs created by the common hammock weaver spider.

Little Miss Muffet, by Sir John Everett Millais.

Spiders

Why do so many people fear spiders and yet are fascinated by and admire the ability of spiders to make beautiful webs? Their silken threads laden with dew festooning fields and hedgerows on an autumn morning is a beautiful sight.

Spiders and their webs feature often in history and literature. Robert the Bruce watched a spider try seven times before it succeeded in securing its web to the ceiling of his cave. Inspired by its perseverance, he decided to try yet again, after his own setbacks, to fight the English.

Five hundred years later Sir Walter Scott wrote about Lord Marmion's lust for Clara de Clare which included the lines:

> *O what a tangled web we weave,*
> *When first we practice to deceive!*

Little Miss Muffet
Sat on a tuffet,
Eating her curds and whey;
Along came a spider,
Who sat down beside her
And frightened Miss Muffet away.

Grasshoppers

The first sight of a grasshopper on a warm summer's day is often when one is startled by their spring-loaded jump from one grass stem to another. They differ from crickets in being diurnal (as opposed to nocturnal) and herbivorous (as opposed to predatory and omnivorous). They make their characteristic chirping song by rubbing a hind leg against their fore wing whilst crickets make it by rubbing their forewings together.

© Petra and Wilfried

Meadow grasshopper.

Craneflies

Craneflies, or daddy-long-legs, are fragile looking insects which have very long legs which are weakly attached to the body and liable to break off. Their larva, called leatherjackets, live in the soil and cause serious damage to grass roots. They are, however, a rich source of food for birds.

They frequently have a synchronised emergence during the early summer which results in large numbers of adults appearing over short periods. Birds take advantage of this abundance to feed their young. In some species a second mass emergence may occur in the autumn. The co-ordinated timing of this is believed to be a survival instinct because predators are not able to multiply sufficiently rapidly to consume a high proportion of the individuals.

© Northeastwildlife.co.uk

Craneflies mating.

Beetles

Beetles are the largest of all the insect groups with more than 4,000 species in Britain. On the Long Mynd over 70 species have been found, each habitat being home for a specific type of beetle. For example, areas of sparse grassland, open paths and bare ground are important for ground beetles such as the metallic green tiger beetle. This handsome beetle is one of the fastest running insects, always on the move in search of prey.

The bloody-nosed beetle is black with a violet tinge and may be found crawling over grass. It is remarkable for its reflex bleeding, exuding a drop of blood from its mouth and various joints when disturbed, a strategy to deter predators, especially birds.

The larval of the hawthorn jewel beetle feed on dead or dying hawthorn. Their D-shaped exit-holes are tell-tale signs which match the cross-section of the adult beetle, flattened on top and convex below.

The heather beetle (page 29) and water beetles (page 41) have already been described.

© Benj Gibbs

© Northeastwildlife.co.uk

Top: Bloody-nosed beetle.   Above: The green tiger beetle.

© Jon Law

© Mark Telfer

Hawthorn jewel beetle and the D-shaped hole it makes as it emerges.

The Old Carding Mill

DOMESDAY BOOK (1086) records that there was a mill at 'Stretton' and it is mentioned again in the manorial records of 1309. It is almost certain that this mill was in what we now call Carding Mill Valley and was probably a water mill for grinding corn powered by the valley stream. The mill belonged to the lord of the manor and in 1563 the then lord of the manor is recorded as selling 'a mill on Nash Brook' to Francis Brooke who soon afterwards rebuilt it. This is likely to have been the same mill as the 'Stretton's mill' referred to in several manorial records of the 1680s and 1690s when it worked in conjunction with a forge. It was probably approached via the track which runs down to Carding Mill Valley from Burway Gate (at the top of Burway Road) rather than along the valley bottom, where the present road is, which was probably marshy and liable to flooding.

Brooks Mill, as it was called, was made of wood with a thatched roof and would have stood adjacent to the Ash Brook, as the stream in the valley is called. The mill was used as a corn or grist mill and worked on a seasonal or occasional basis. Together with an old cottage, they were the only buildings in the valley. On 27th May 1811 after torrential rain, there was widespread flooding throughout south Shropshire and many people were drowned. It is believed that the mill was swept away by flood waters.

A substantial new three storey mill was then erected close by but well above the valley floor by the Rev'd George Watkin Marsh, Rector of Hope Bowdler. It was originally intended as a corn mill but as there was a carding mill at All Stretton (Dagers mill, later called Dudgeley mill), the functions of the two buildings were exchanged and the new mill in the valley became a carding mill and at the same time gave the valley this new name.

The mill and mill wheel prior to demolition about 1913.

The mill stood at an angle of about 30° to the valley road and had a 16 ft diameter water wheel situated at the south end of the building. The mill was powered by water brought by a leat (channel) from a series of mill pools higher up the valley which drove an undershot wheel which worked the machinery inside.[3] Initially, there was one mill pool below Cow Ridge collecting water from Cow Ridge Gutter (now called New Pool Hollow). A second collecting pool was created above the existing one below Cow Ridge and was called the New Pool, so giving the name New Pool Hollow to this side valley.[4] A third pool on the site of the present upper car park in Mill Glen, as the Carding Mill Valley was then called,[5] collected water from the Ash Brook and was connected via wooden troughs and a channel to the original pool. Together, these supplied the

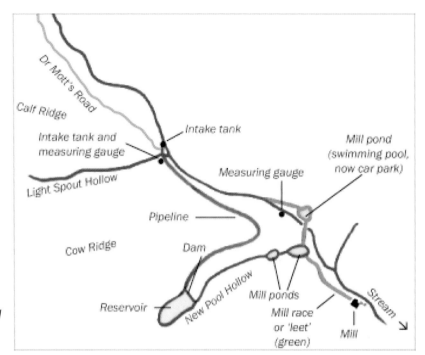

Plan showing the water gathering arrangements for the mill in the Carding Mill Valley and the New Pool Hollow reservoir (built 1902).

© Barrie Raynor

© Barrie Raynor

Left: The water channel linking the mill pool in Carding Mill valley where the upper car park is now and the lower of the two mill pools in New Pool Hollow, looking north towards the car park.
Right: The two mill pools in New Pool Hollow viewed from Cow Ridge. It is likely that the mill pools were also used by the miller as a fishery to generate further income.

water for the 4–5 m wide leat behind the mill. The remains of these two mill pools can still be seen at the foot of New Pool Hollow, albeit both much smaller and constrained by concrete weirs.

The original function of the mill was to card wool, that is combing out the tangle of fibres from a fleece using a series of belts and rollers with spikes so that the wool fibres were aligned. The wool was then wound loosely on to cards ready for spinning by women and children in their own homes. The carding mill greatly increased the supply of wool to the hand spinners and weavers, providing in one hour the amount of wool that would have taken a week to card by hand.

The first tenant of the rebuilt mill was a Lancashire man, Ashworth Pilkington, but the business was not successful and the Rev'd Marsh then worked the mill with his brother-in-law, a Mr Booth, a retired naval officer who was brought in to run the operation and supervise the workers. Booth lived in two rooms in the basement, sleeping in a hammock.

In 1824 George Corfield of Little Stretton bought the mill. He also bought a piece of land alongside the mill and built a large new building, commonly called 'The Factory' facing the brook and installed hand looms and spinning jennies to produce cloth on the upper two floors in an open space 60 ft x 24 ft. The ground floor was fitted out as

The building at the back of this photo, taken about 1890, is the mill. The large building in the centre is the 'factory' built by George Corfield in 1824 to house the spinning jennies and looms. It has since been converted into flats. The house in the foreground was the mill manager's house and is now the home, much altered, of the National Trust Warden.

four cottages for employees. This is the present large three-storey building facing the stream now converted into six flats. About this time, a building providing stables and storage space was built on the other side of the Ash Brook. This has since been converted into a house, Mill View. The mill manager's house next to the factory was probably built about the same time.

For a number of years George Corfield and his son, George, made a success of the business. However the size of the enterprise was small and eventually

Originally, carding was done by children using teasel brushes but later a pair of hand carding-bats was used to straighten out and untangle the fibres and remove detritus from the mass of raw wool. The cards were wooden blocks with handles and covered in wire spikes which were set in leather. Carding was a slow and labour-intensive process and eventually machines were made to speed up this stage which had held up the spinning and weaving of cloth.

In July each year, Church Stretton held an annual wool market under the Market Hall in the High Street. Wool would be sold as raw fleeces or already carded and cottagers would bring their spun yarns for sale.

failed due to competition from the more mechanised steam-powered mills in Lancashire and Yorkshire and the effect of the commercial depression of the 1830s. George Corfield senior died in 1837 and a Mr Evans from Newtown soon took over the mill but he died in 1845.

The 1841 census gives a clear picture for the first time of how many people were employed at the mill and in what capacity. There were ten males and two females, including two wool pickers, a sorter, two yarn slubbers (people who removed imperfections in the yarn), a carding engine feeder, two spinners and two flannel weavers. These people lived with their families, some on the premises and others in several cottages in the valley. After Evans' death, Thomas Duppa and a Mr Banks leased the mill, calling it the Long Mynd Mills. By 1851 their labour force

had grown to 19, all having been brought in from Newtown where there was a long established woollen industry.

In 1854 James Williams, who had been the manager for George Corfield, became tenant of the mill but also lost money and employed only seven workers in 1861. The scale of the business declined further and after James Williams' death in 1866, the business was carried on by his son Richard manufacturing tweed cloth, blankets and rugs with only six employees recorded in the 1871 census. The mill and the factory were put up for sale in 1870 (see poster overleaf) but it seems that there was no buyer.

Between 1881 and about 1906 the Church Stretton Aerated Water Company, owned by three Goodwin brothers, operated in an extension to the front of the mill building and from the factory building, using water from one of the Long Mynd springs to produce a selection of drinks such as soda water, lemonade and ginger beer (see page 144).

Tragedy again struck the valley during the 11–14th May 1886 when another torrential storm which continued for three days and nights deposited over 4½ ins of rain. Filled to overflowing by the constant rain, the two large mill pools in New Pool Hollow used for the storage of water to drive the mill wheel burst their massive dams and sent a cascade of water through the valley and into Church Stretton.[6] It is not known what damage was done to the mill and factory but soon afterwards the Goodwin brothers bought the mill and factory.

Throughout this period, Richard Williams continued to manufacture cloth in the factory building and by the 1890s he was advertising tweed and blankets and offering to provide cloth to farmers in exchange for wool. In addition, his wife opened refreshment rooms on the ground floor to serve the tourists who were beginning to visit Church Stretton and the Carding Mill Valley in large numbers.

Although wool was still being woven into rugs and thick grey cloth in 1904, Williams' business was becoming unprofitable and was forced to close within a year or two. With no buyer the mill fell into disrepair and was demolished about 1913 and the old factory was converted into a hotel and café.

CHURCH STRETTON,
SALOP.

PARTICULARS OF VALUABLE

FREEHOLD PROPERTY

TO BE SOLD BY AUCTION,

BY

MR. EDWARD HEIGHWAY,

AT THE

Hotel, Church Stretton,

ON TUESDAY, THE 29TH DAY OF NOVEMBER, 1870,

At THREE o'Clock in the Afternoon precisely, and subject to Conditions of Sale to be then produced,

All that Substantially-built

WOOLLEN FACTORY
AND CARDING MILL,

WITH

DYE-HOUSE, WALK-MILL & DRYING FRAMES, WORKSHOP, WORKMEN'S COTTAGES, MANAGER'S RESIDENCE and GARDEN,

MEADOW & PASTURE LANDS,

Containing in the whole 7 a. 1 r. 37 p. (more or less) situate in the MILL GLEN, about half-a-mile from Church Stretton.

Mr. Williams, the Tenant, will shew the Property, and for lithographed plans and particulars, apply to the Auctioneer, All Stretton, Salop, or to Mr. Marston, Solicitor, Ludlow.

Poster for the auction of the mill properties in 1870.

Mrs. Williams,
Carding Mill,
Church Stretton,

BEGS to inform the Excursionists who visit this charming locality that she supplies TEA AND OTHER REFRESHMENTS at very moderate charges. Special arrangements made for Choirs, Schools and Large Parties. The Carding Mill is situated in the beautiful and romantic Carding Mill Valley, half-way between Church Stretton and the far-famed Light Spout.

Full Particulars on application.

THOROUGHLY RENOVATED THROUGHOUT.

Mrs Williams, wife of Richard Williams opened a café in the carding mill premises. This is her advertisement from 1905.

A bungalow was built on the site of the mill. A prefabricated wooden chalet imported from Scandinavia was erected just before 1905 and was used for accommodation by the manager.[7] Thereafter, the hotel and café and later the Chalet Pavilion (imported about 1920) became the focal point for streams of tourists who arrived in charabancs and cars.

William Ernest Gordon Pearce (pictured) bought the mill and the hotel and café and much of Carding Mill Valley in 1920. He opened refreshment rooms in the Chalet Pavilion in addition to his existing premises in Church Stretton. Pearce (and later his son Stanley) continued to run the Carding Mill Valley premises until 1959 when his son sold the hotel and café and later the rest of Carding Mill Valley, to Harold Holmes. The hotel and café were converted into flats in 1970 and called Carding Mill Court. The National Trust bought the chalet, Chalet Pavilion and the valley from him in 1979.

There were other mills in the area. In All Stretton there are records of mills from 1599 and 1663 but it is uncertain whether these are the same mill as Dagers mill which eventually became known as Dudgeley mill and which was operational until 1917. In Little Stretton there was a mill called Lytyleston mill on Ashes Brook in 1327 and another on Callow brook called Oakley or Hockley mill, the evidence for which is derived from local field names. On the Quinny brook near the Acton Scott boundary there was the Quenbatch mill, first recorded in 1392. Later it became known as Queensbatch mill and continued in operation milling corn until 1951.

© Royal Mail

This postage stamp of Carding Mill Valley (looking east towards Church Stretton) with associated hand stamp was issued in 2006 as one of the British Journeys series.

© David Austin Roses Ltd

The rose 'Carding Mill'.

© Tony Crowe Collection

The Queensbatch corn mill in 1905 shows the miller James Edwards and his wife Mary with his three employees.

This postcard is postmarked 1905 and shows the buildings in the valley before the Chalet Pavilion was built. Part of the premises of the Church Stretton Aerated Water Co. can be seen in front of the original mill at the back of the photo. The chalet in the foreground is now part of the National Trust offices.

Carding Mill Hotel and Café in about 1920 before the Chalet Pavilion was built. Notice the National petrol pump, the weighing machine to its left and the various penny slot machines such as 'What the Butler Saw' and 'Horse Racing' by the roadside.

The wool was dyed on the 'Factory' premises using the local natural plant dyes. Judging by the colours in a couple of rugs still in existence, one shown here, the red dye was likely to be from the local bilberries. Gorse flowers and blackberries would produce other colours.

The Chalet Pavilion   Carding Mill Valley, Church Stretton

Open Daily (Sundays included)

The best accommodation in the District for Parties.

Noted for

High Class Catering

For Large or Small Parties.

Satisfaction guaranteed.

References with pleasure.

The Pavilion is surrounded by delightful hill scenery, in the beautiful Carding Mill Valley, just off the Shrewsbury to Hereford Main Road. Easy run for Char-a-bancs, &c., up to the doors.

Lavatories and Cloak-rooms, Lock-up Cycle Store, &c.   Seating accommodation for over 200.

Quotations for Hot or Cold Luncheons, Teas, &c., for Works-Outings, Private Parties, Choirs, Sunday Schools, &c., on application to

Miss Wyke, The Chalet, Carding Mill Valley, Church Stretton.

Above: A 1920s postcard showing the warehouse and factory converted into a hotel and café. The ground floor had kitchens at the rear and penny slot machines at the front. The first floor was the café and the top floor the hotel. The adjoining house in the foreground, much altered, was originally the mill manager's house. The bungalow at the back was built on the site of the mill.

Above: A 1922 advertisement for the newly built Chalet Pavilion café managed, and later owned, by Florence Wyke.

The Chalet Pavilion restaurant after Harold Holmes bought it in 1946.

Tourism

The Church Stretton Posting Establishment in Burway Road, 1908.

THE COMING of the railway to Church Stretton in 1852 encouraged visitors, especially the well-to-do, to spend a day in the town and the local countryside to take the air, the water, walks and tours around the area. Victorian doctors recommended that their patients come to the hills for rest and recovery. By 1880, railway companies were providing special excursion trains from the West Midlands and Lancashire to Church Stretton especially at weekends and during the wakes-week holidays. Visitors would walk from the station to Carding Mill Valley bringing with them a picnic and spend the afternoon picking bilberries. August Bank holidays often saw 800 visitors arrive on special excursion trains.

From the 1870s, some visitors made use of the riding and carriage facilities provided by the Church Stretton Posting Establishment where they could hire saddle horses, hunters, ponies and dog-carts as well as a range of horse-drawn carriages such as Landaus, Victorias (with rubber tyres) and Brakes. A list of recommended rides complete with timing and a tariff was published in local guidebooks.

In the first guidebook to Church Stretton published in 1885, the following advice was given:

> *'Before ascending Longmynd, the visitor should remember, nothing is to be obtained on its summit save water. Ladies should always carry a camp stool, and gentlemen will find a stout stick or Alpen stock of great utility. A drinking cup is also a very useful thing to carry, and some sandwiches are really required. A light waterproof is a very useful thing as storms sometimes arise most unexpectedly in these elevated regions. No one need be afraid of anything venomous, snakes are unknown; the most fearful antagonist will be a bee culling honey from the golden gorse.'*

© Bernard Ford

This party in a four-in-hand carriage from The Feathers Hotel, *Ludlow led by Mr Goodwin is seen on the Long Mynd in June 1900.*

© Tony Crowe Collection

© Barrie Raynor

The large mill pool in Carding Mill Valley was used for many years from the 1900s as an outdoor bathing pool and in the winter for skating by the local residents and visitors, hence the sign which still stands near the spot saying 'Depth opposite this point 3 ft 10 ins'. The pool was drained in about 1960 and filled to be used as a car park.

After the First World War, the charabanc outing began to replace the rail excursion. These open-topped vehicles were commonly hired for church and Sunday school outings. The early charabancs had solid tyres and the ride would have been very hard and bumpy. They had a clumsy canvas hood stowed at the rear which could be used when it rained.

At Easter in 1938 the increased use of the motor car resulted in complaints being made about day-trippers from the Black

Charabancs in Carding Mill Valley in the late 1920s. The front charabanc is a Dennis (c.1919). Notice the carbide and oil lamps. The tyres were solid rubber and the body would have been made by a separate coachbuilder.

An Edwardian family outing to Carding Mill Valley complete with picnic basket.

Mrs Rose Emily Goodwin and her mother, Mrs Jones, and spaniel in the Carding Mill Valley about 1889.

Country who, with their kegs of beer, were held to be responsible for the 'fairground' appearance of the valley. This probably represented the height of the valley's popularity and its attendant conflicts with local people. Tea wars broke out between the competing establishments chasing patrons in the valley for parking charges and patronage. The Pavilion Tea Rooms could seat 250 and became a favourite rendezvous for works outings, social and sports clubs and Sunday school parties. On one occasion in 1914, cafés in Church Stretton and Carding Mill Valley served over 3,000 breakfasts to the Liverpool based Bibby Shipping Line's work's outing which came in five special trains.

In an attempt to improve the class of clientele visiting the district, the Church Stretton Advancement Association began promoting the town as a superior climatic resort with good golfing and provided a park and recreation grounds in the town for visitors and entertainment by bandsmen near to the hotels. The town was also promoted as a winter resort where hotel residents could enjoy the activities and fayres associated with an alpine resort, the winters then being much harsher than at present. Amazingly, the British Alpine Society held their annual four-day Easter break here in 1905!

© Yvonne Beaumont

The Long Mynd was promoted on railway posters using slogans like *The Highlands of England, Little Switzerland, The British Shangri-la* and the Light Spout waterfall was *England's Little Niagara.*

Nowadays, there are still large numbers of tourists who come all the year round, especially at the weekend and bank holidays and during the school holidays. On these occasions the valley can be saturated with cars. The National Trust's policy is to attract visitors to just one of the Long Mynd valleys so as to take the pressure off other valleys and the hill, allowing them to be enjoyed by visitors seeking more peace and solitude.

The Light Spout Waterfall.

The Longmynd Hotel

The hotel was originally built with a tiled gabled roof.

THIS HOTEL was built in 1901 originally as *The Hydropathic Hotel* in half timbered style with a fine pitched roof containing two rows of dormer windows probably to fit into the landscape of the late Victorian housing developments. It stood in its own grounds of about nine acres and was furnished by Heal's of London and offered tennis, billiards, croquet and golf to its residents. *The Hydro* made an auspicious start with a celebratory dinner in July 1901 with 35 guests travelling in a special coach attached to the 2.40 pm train from Paddington. Initially, as a hydropathic establishment, the hotel brought water by train from Llandrindod Wells.

In 1908 the Church Stretton Land Company had an ambitious scheme to develop the town by buying the hotel, enlarging it to accommodate 120–130 visitors and piping water from a saline spring near Wentnor to a new pump room, promenade and gardens to be built in the grounds of Woodcote nearby. The Wentnor spring potentially yielded 600 gallons a day and the plan was to pump the water through 1½ in. glass-enamelled wrought iron pipes to an underground tank holding 1,000 gallons located near Pole Bank. From there the water would flow by gravity to the pump room. This all came to nothing because of the cost of construction, doubts about whether the water actually had any medicinal benefits (it had no sulphur or iron) and the general declining interest in spas. Besides, the water was a powerful laxative and best drunk not too far from home! As

a result, the *Hydropathic Hotel* was soon renamed *Longmynd Hotel!* The Company also had plans for a funicular railway up to the hotel similar to that at Bridgnorth but that also came to nought.

In the early 1920s the hotel was altered to the existing design by the removal of the pitched roof and dormer windows and their replacement with a flat roof.

An advertisement from Church Stretton Illustrated, *1905.*

The rear terrace in the 1920s.

Longmynd Hotel in 1954.

New Pool Hollow Reservoir

Church Stretton Water Supply and Reservoirs

THE LARGE number of natural springs on the plateau has always provided a ready supply of fresh water for settlements around the Long Mynd. The stream down Townbrook Valley was probably a major factor in bringing the first settlers to Church Stretton. It is almost certain that during the Anglo Saxon and early Norman periods 'Stratun', as it was referred to in the Domesday Book (1086), was sited adjacent to the Town Brook at the foot of Burway Road where the Old Rectory and Pryll Cottage now stand. It had a population then of between 140 and 175 persons.

With increased prosperity as a market centre for the Long Mynd sheep and ponies, the centre of gravity of the town moved to the area around what is now the Market Square. From the seventeenth century, the Town Brook, which at the time ran down the middle of what is now the lower part of Burway Road and Sandford Avenue, became used as a source of water for malting and fellmongering businesses. Both of these processes are smelly and produce by-products which polluted the brook. This, together with the increasing population of the town in the 19th century brought about by its importance as a market centre, necessitated a cleaner and more reliable supply of water which the local springs and the Town Brook could not supply.

© Barrie Raynor

The first reservoir was in Townbrook Valley. It still exists as an attractive pool full of trout.

The Townbrook Valley Reservoir

To provide for a better supply of water, the Church Stretton Water Company was formed in 1857. It constructed a small reservoir (about 150,000 gallons) in Townbrook Valley (or Black Valley, as it was once known[8]) from which a piped water supply went to the town.

By the end of the 19th century, Church Stretton was growing rapidly. Its population had already exceeded 600 which was raised in the summer season when the town was invaded by long-stay visitors. Unlike many of the local residents, these visitors from the large cities expected flushing lavatories and increasingly, plumbed baths. The reservoir became inadequate and a severe drought in the summer of 1898 during which the supply of water was restricted to 3 hours each day, necessitated an urgent solution. In 1899, Parliament passed the Church Stretton Water Act to establish another water company, the Church Stretton Waterworks Company, with a capital of £20,000 to be raised by the issue of shares and stock. The new company purchased the original Church Stretton Water Company and the separate Little Stretton Waterworks Company and became responsible for the water supply to the three Strettons.

New Pool Hollow Reservoir as it is now after reduction in the height of the dam.

New Pool Hollow Reservoir

Between 1899 and 1902 the Church Stretton Waterworks Company company replaced the smaller reservoir in Townbrook Valley by a new reservoir built in New Pool Hollow, a side valley of the Carding Mill Valley. This had a much larger capacity of about 14 million gallons and supplied water to Church Stretton and Little Stretton but not All Stretton. It was officially opened on the 25th October 1902 before it was fully full.

The reservoir contained water gathered from other side valleys further up Carding Mill Valley, especially the Light Spout Hollow. Near where this stream meets the main stream, an intake tank was installed from which water was piped around the hillside into the reservoir. Some of these pipes from the Light Spout Hollow can still be seen exposed above the ground.

The Company installed measuring gauges at various points to ensure a minimum flow of water in the Carding Mill stream of 62,500 gallons every 24 hours. The remains of such gauges can be seen about 30 m above the top car park, a second gauge is in the Light Spout Hollow about 50 m above its confluence with the main stream and a third above the New Pool Hollow reservoir.

From a height of approximately 1,000 feet above sea level, the supply of water from the reservoir reached most of the properties in the town at that time by gravity.

How do the water gauges work?

The rate of flow depends on the angle of the V-shaped notch and the height of the water surface flowing through the notch. For a 90° notch angle, the flow rate is proportional to the height raised to the power $^5/_2$. Actual flow rates can easily be measured once the device has been calibrated.

One of the measuring gauges still remaining in Carding Mill Valley and New Pool Hollow.

The water company was acquired by the Church Stretton Urban District Council in 1912, then in 1964 by the West Shropshire Water Board which later became part of the Severn Trent Water Board and from 1990 part of the Severn Trent Water Company.

The water from the New Pool Hollow reservoir was piped direct to the houses without treatment. In the light of increased standards for purity, it was found to contain biological and mineral pollutants and was declared unsafe to drink without further treatment. During a hot spell in 1976 over 75 people were found swimming in the reservoir! This hastened further the closure of the reservoir and a piped water supply from the treatment works on the River Severn at Shelton, Shrewsbury was built the following year.

Beneath the dam embankment lies the reservoir access tunnel. Two teams of Welsh miners had been employed to dig the 400 ft tunnel which leads from the base of the control tower to beyond the dam wall. This tunnel was cut through rock and was provided so that the reservoir could be emptied at times of emergency or when maintenance was needed. Running along inside the tunnel is the original cast iron pipe which supplied the town. For engineering and safety reasons the height of the dam was substantially reduced in 1978 when the ownership was transferred to the National Trust.

Prior to 1902, Little Stretton had been served by a small reservoir at the foot of Small Batch, the remains of which can be seen next to a row of pine trees.

The small reservoir in The Batch, in the foreground above, served All Stretton until 1977 when the piped supply from Shrewsbury reached the Strettons. It was owned by the All Stretton Parish Council Water Works Co. This photograph was taken in 1960.

© Tony Crowe Collection

Bottled Water Companies

THE CHURCH Stretton guide book of 1895 stated:

Church Stretton has achieved considerable notoriety for the unrivalled excellence of its water supply and the marvellous purity of its water which is possibly the finest and purest drinking water available.

The water referred to came from springs on the Long Mynd and was exploited by two companies.

The Church Stretton Aerated Water Company

This was the first mineral water company to start operating in Church Stretton. It started in business in 1881 in an extension to the old mill building in Carding Mill Valley, drawing water from a nearby spring. It was owned by the Goodwin brothers, William John, Harry Orton and Harold. The company sold soda, seltzer, lithia and potassium waters, ginger ale and lemonade. It seemed to have ceased trading by 1906.

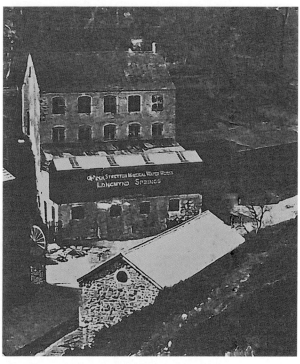

The Church Stretton Mineral Water Works used the trade name 'Longmynd Springs'. It operated in an extension to the front of the mill and in a new building to the right. Note the stables in the stone building in the foreground. Postcard about 1905.

Purest Water in England!

☞ *See Analysis.*

Goodwin's Longmynd Stretton Waters.

To be had at all London Clubs, and of leading Wine Merchants and Chemists, or wholesale from the

Manufactory—CHURCH STRETTON, SHROPSHIRE.

Bemrose, Typ., Derb

Church Stretton Aerated Water Company bottles.

THE
CHURCH STRETTON AERATED WATER
COMPANY

Take this opportunity of thanking the inhabitants of Church Stretton, and of the County of Salop generally, for the liberal support which has been accorded to them during the season.

They wish at the same time to express their determination to manufacture none but the highest quality of Aerated Drinks, and in this way they hope to sustain the reputation for extreme purity which the water of the Longmynd District has so justly acquired.

SODA WATER	LEMONADE
POTASH ,,	GINGER BEER
SELTZER ,,	GINGER ALE
LITHIA ,,	CHAMPAGNE CYDER.

All made from pure filtered
LONGMYND WATER.

AGENT : MR. W. B. PAYNE, Church Stretton.

An 1881 advertisement in the Church Stretton Times.

The Stretton Hills Mineral Water Company

This is located in Shrewsbury Road. It was the larger of the two companies. Charles Hince opened it in 1883 in a purpose built factory using the Cound Dale spring. The 1901 OS map refers to it for the first time as Cwm Dale. Perhaps the change in name was at the instigation of the mineral water company who thought it a more prestigious one.

The Company was described in 1893 as
manufacturing every description of mineral and aerated waters, including soda water, potassium water, seltzer water, lithia water, Vichy water, quinine water, lemonade, ginger beer, ginger ale, lime fruit, juice champagne, original barm ginger beer, and puts Cwm Dale Spring pure water into pint or quart bottles.

During the 1880s and 1890s all advertisements emphasised the purity of this water which together with the pure air of Church Stretton were specially recommended for curing or alleviating many ailments including 'neuresthenia, influenza, sleeplessness, delicate children, amnesia, general debility, weak digestion, catarrh, obesity, etc.'

Stretton Hills Mineral Water Co. Ltd

The glass bottle dates from the 1890s.
Henry Reddin was a wine and spirit merchant in Church Stretton from 1888 to 1905 and had his own ginger beer stoneware bottles personally transfer-labelled.
Jewsbury & Brown owned the company from about 1926.

The reputation of Cwm Dale water grew and it was widely exported. Throughout the British Empire the best hotels and clubs stocked Stretton Water. Queen Victoria was apparently so impressed by its quality that she decreed that the Governors of our Colonies should enjoy a regular supply of Stretton Water.

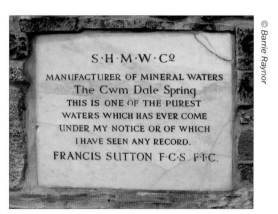

© Barrie Raynor

S·H·M·W·C°

MANUFACTURER OF MINERAL WATERS
The Cwm Dale Spring
THIS IS ONE OF THE PUREST WATERS WHICH HAS EVER COME UNDER MY NOTICE OR OF WHICH I HAVE SEEN ANY RECORD.
FRANCIS SUTTON F·C·S F·I·C·

The comments by the eminent analytical chemist Francis Sutton are recorded on a stone plaque incorporated in the front wall of the works.

At first the Company used water from the spring behind the factory, stored in a large underground settling tank built of white glazed brick holding about 70,000 gallons. The water was piped directly into the plant under gravity, any excess feeding the tap in the wall at the roadside. This source of water

is no longer used, though in 1985 Cwm Dale Spring water was approved as a distinct and registered brand.

In 2000 the older parts of the works were demolished and replaced with a modern building which allowed production to be increased and the plant to meet modern hygiene requirements.

To supply increasing demand for Stretton's bottled water it is now pumped from the aquifer in the Stretton valley. The company supplies water to several retailers. So that each brand can claim to have a unique water source with a distinct mineral analysis, the water is pumped from four separate bore holes located in the fields opposite. They are over 25 m deep and penetrate the glacial deposits on the valley floor, thus the water does not now come *directly* from the Long Mynd.

The original company was eventually acquired by Jewsbury & Brown Ltd. and is now owned by Princes Soft Drinks.

"Stretton"
English Natural Table Water

BOTTLED AT THE
CELEBRATED CWM SPRING.

"A purer and better table Table Water could not be desired."—JOHN C. TRESH, M.D., D.SC.

"For gouty people the Cwm Spring is specially suited owing to its peculiar freedom from lime and other dissolved mineral matters."—W. N. THURSFIELD, M.D.

"This is one of the purest natural Waters which has ever come under my notice or of which I have seen any record."—FRANCIS SUTTON, F.C.S., F.I.C.

IN BOTTLES, HALF-BOTTLES, AND SPLITS.
To be obtained at all the chief Hotels and Stores in London and the Provinces.

The Stretton Hills Mineral Water Co.,
CHURCH STRETTON, SHROPSHIRE,
MANUFACTURERS OF
SODA WATER, LEMONADE, GINGER ALE, DRY GINGER ALE, GINGER BEER, Etc.
In the preparation of which the Cwm Spring water is used.

An advertisement from 1922.

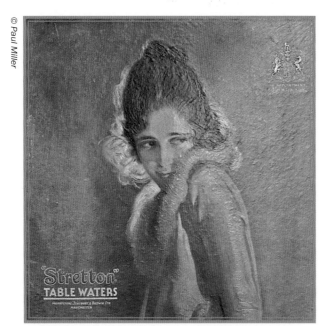

The Queen Mother's portrait by David Jagger was used in a 1953 advertisement.

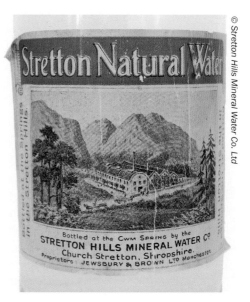

Bottle label showing the 'mountainous' Stretton Hills!

Advertising plaque.

Cwm Dale

Cwm Dale was called Cound Dale until about 1893 and must have been considered as the source of the Cound Brook which flows northwards to join the Severn at Lower Cound near Attingham Park, despite the Ash Brook in Carding Mill Valley being longer and having a greater volume water. It could be that because of the watershed between the north and south flowing rivers in the Stretton Gap is very flat, the Ash Brook once flowed south to join the Town Brook. As a result, it would naturally be thought that the spring in Cound (Cwm) Dale was the source of the Cound Brook. To the east of Cwmdale and separating it from the Stretton valley is the prominent Nover's Hill. On it are the remains of a small triangular enclosure and the foundations of a building of medieval or post-medieval date. Cwmdale is also he site of an ancient Saxon pen, an enclosure being the homestead of an extended family and their livestock. The field boundaries can still be seen from Nover's Hill at certain times of the year.

Pole Bank

THE HIGHEST point on the Long Mynd is Pole Bank which the Ordnance Survey records having a height of 516 m. It is little more than a gentle heather-covered mound with a trig point and toposcope on it to distinguish it from other nearby mounds and barrows. It lies about 200 m from the Portway near where the old Church Stretton to Medlicott drove road crosses it. On the 1752 map by Rocque, it is referred to as The Pole, though Robert Baugh's map of 1808 does not mention it. Estate maps of 1828, 1831 and 1834 call the mound Pole Bank and the highest point Shepherd's Pole. It may be that a pole had been erected as a guide post for travellers in an area where it is very easy to lose one's bearings when the Long Mynd is blanketed by snow.

This pole must have fallen, for in 1860, the Ordnance Survey erected a new one. This was replaced again on the 6th September 1927 by Dr E S Cobbold with a 40 ft pole which mysteriously disappeared in 1935.[9] The lord of the manor, Max Wenner, was suspected of removing it because it was attracting too many walkers who were disturbing his grouse shooting.

The toposcope was erected in 1986 to commemorate the diamond jubilee of the founding of the Council for the Protection of Rural England.

Pole Cottage

About 500 m to the south of Pole Bank there used to lie the isolated Pole Cottage on the west side of the Portway surrounded by little fields and several ponds. The cottage has now been pulled down but the enclosed field is bounded by mature beech, hazel and Scots pine with an undercover of heather. At one stage it had been a farm with several outbuildings and anecdotal evidence suggests that a few hundred years ago it was an inn, perhaps not surprising since

Pole Bank: The trig point and the toposcope.

it would have been a useful refuge in the days when the Portway was a busy trading route.[10] In the 19th and 20th centuries, it was a home at times to shepherds and gamekeepers who worked on the moor.

The first recorded occupant was John Matthews, probably a shepherd or gamekeeper employed by the estate of the Earl of Powis in 1828. The property was referred to as *Shepherd's Lodge* on Mickleburgh's estate map of 1834, a name by which it continued to be known in the 1851, 1861 and 1871 censuses. In those years, it was occupied by Thomas Gwilliam and his family. After the Ordnance Survey re-erected the pole on Pole Bank in 1860 the property has usually been called Pole Cottage.

The cottage was occupied for many years by a beekeeping hermit and the last inhabitant, who also had the right also to turn out thirty sheep, was Edward Crebbin with whom the right expired after he retired about 1911. Arthur Evans succeeded him in Pole Cottage and was employed as a gamekeeper for the then lord of the manor, Lord Alexander Thynne. The property was occupied by a refugee during the 2nd World War.

© NT Shropshire Hills

Arthur Evans with his dog Diddleums at Pole Cottage, 1918.

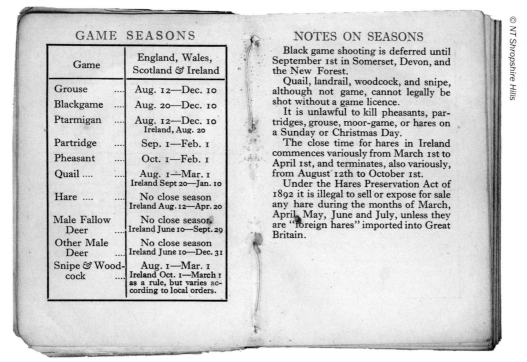

© NT Shropshire Hills

GAME SEASONS

Game	England, Wales, Scotland & Ireland
Grouse	Aug. 12—Dec. 10
Blackgame	Aug. 20—Dec. 10
Ptarmigan	Aug. 12—Dec. 10 Ireland, Aug. 20
Partridge	Sep. 1—Feb. 1
Pheasant	Oct. 1—Feb. 1
Quail	Aug. 1—Mar. 1 Ireland Sept 20—Jan. 10
Hare	No close season Ireland Aug. 12—Apr. 20
Male Fallow Deer	No close season Ireland June 10—Sept. 29
Other Male Deer	No close season Ireland June 10—Dec. 31
Snipe & Woodcock	Aug. 1—Mar. 1 Ireland Oct. 1—March 1 as a rule, but varies according to local orders.

NOTES ON SEASONS

Black game shooting is deferred until September 1st in Somerset, Devon, and the New Forest.

Quail, landrail, woodcock, and snipe, although not game, cannot legally be shot without a game licence.

It is unlawful to kill pheasants, partridges, grouse, moor-game, or hares on a Sunday or Christmas Day.

The close time for hares in Ireland commences variously from March 1st to April 1st, and terminates, also variously, from August 12th to October 1st.

Under the Hares Preservation Act of 1892 it is illegal to sell or expose for sale any hare during the months of March, April, May, June and July, unless they are "foreign hares" imported into Great Britain.

Two pages from Arthur Evans' 1923 Shooter's Year Book Diary. *Reference is made to black game (black grouse) and landrail (corncrake) which would have been common on the Long Mynd then.*

Falconry on the Long Mynd

IN MEDIEVAL times when the Long Mynd was a royal forest, royal falconers (including, it is said, King John) hunted a wide range of game birds with hawks and falcons. In the nineteenth and early twentieth centuries, the Long Mynd became a popular shooting moor for sportsmen following the introduction of a few pairs of grouse from

William Humphrey with his golden eagle Circa.

William Goodwin with his falcon at the Carding Mill, about 1900.

Yorkshire about 1840 by William Pinches of Ticklerton and his brother-in-law the Rev'd R J Buddicom. By the 1930s, bags of 100 brace a day were not uncommon and the Long Mynd became one of the manor's most desirable assets.

An early falconer on the hill was William Goodwin, one of the Goodwin brothers who owned the mineral water company at the Carding Mill during the period 1881–1906. In more recent years William Humphrey, landlord of the *Stiperstones Inn,* owned the Long Mynd as lord of the manor from 1937 to 1963. He was an experienced, albeit eccentric, falconer and flew his golden eagle called *Circa* on the hill. He is particularly remembered for breeding and improving the Llewellin setter, a popular and successful breed of sporting dog.

Ronald Stevens

The most well-known falconer was Ronald Stevens, who with his younger brother Noel owned Walcot Hall in Lydbury North from 1933. He rented the Long Mynd from Humphrey in 1937 to fly his two peregrine falcons. That first year he bagged 33 grouse, 3 pheasants, 4 duck, a partridge, a kestrel and a wood pigeon. Stevens and his guests would be driven up to the moor each day by his brother in his open-top Rolls Royce

Noel Stevens (with Andean goose), Emperor Haile Selassie and Ronald Stevens at Walcot Hall, 1938.

Ronald Stevens on the Long Mynd, 1958.

Falconers Jack Mavrogordato (2nd from left), Ronald Stevens (3rd), William Humphrey (5th) with his Llewellin setters and Charles Binney, assistant secretary of the Kennel Club (right) at Pole Cottage in the early 1950s.

loaded with hawks, lunch boxes and bottles. He was to become one of the foremost exponents of the sport and wrote four books on the subject.

One important visitor was Emperor Haile Selassie of Abyssinia (now Ethiopia). He was a keen falconer and during his exile in England (1936–1941) he visited the Stevens brothers in Walcot Hall and joined them in flying falcons on the Long Mynd.

During the 2nd World War, the RAF used 15 falcons, officially known as Interceptor Unit No. 2, to patrol the wild reaches of the English Channel. The falcons were trained by Ronald Stevens to down carrier pigeons which had been trained by the Germans to carry messages to secret agents in England. They were credited with having a significant disruptive effect upon Hitler's cross-channel spy service. However the falcons could not distinguish between British and German carrier pigeons and the project had to be abandoned! He later said his wartime falcons were so wedded to pigeons that they would not take grouse and he had to train fresh birds. After the war he also trained peregrine falcons at RAF Shawbury where they successfully dispersed flocks of birds from the airfield.[10]

The King of Buganda with Noel and Ronald Stevens (on the right) at Walcot Hall.

Stevens rebuilt Pole Cottage and the outbuildings and lived there from August to December each year with another professional falconer, Frank Muirden, and Mrs Cadwallader their housekeeper. He renamed the property *Frog's Gutter*, it being the traditional name given to the area. The cottage was described as 'just like camping but with a roof on' yet it became a pilgrimage for many well known falconers who stayed there. He also dug several more decoy ponds behind the cottage to encourage the wild duck. By 1954 Ronald Stevens and Geoffrey Pollard, another annual visitor, had between them the largest collection of game hawks in the country, consisting of 2 gyr falcons, 5 peregrine falcons, a merlin and a goshawk, all of which were pegged out behind Pole Cottage.

Another special visitor to Walcot Hall in August 1955 was the King of Buganda, Frederic Musela II who was taken to the Long Mynd by William Humphreys to see his and Ronald Stevens' peregrines in action and to shoot grouse.

1955 was the last season to see trained hawks on the Long Mynd; droves of motorists and hikers were getting in the way and the moor had deteriorated due to encroaching bracken. Ronald Stevens decided to leave Shropshire for Ireland, being attracted by the hawking possibilities around Connemarra.

The cottage was used for several years afterwards as summer accommodation for RSPB wardens who were protecting nesting merlins. This was not the end of Pole Cottage, however, as it continued to be the focal point for the annual event of sheep dipping. All the sheep had to be taken off the hill to be dipped and their owners would then trudge back up to Pole Cottage and have a good time there while the police, in uniform, checked the hillsides for any remaining sheep. Their work done, they would join in the party too! After some years the police were relieved of this duty and the event died out.

In the 1970s, following an accidental fire, the cottage was demolished by the National Trust, leaving only a corrugated iron shed close to the site. In 1990 grouse shooting which had recommenced after Stevens' departure to Ireland was banned on the Long Mynd.

© NT Shropshire Hills

One of several ponds behind Pole Cottage which had been excavated around 1900, reputedly dug by the Earl of Powys, then lord of the manor of Medlicott, as a shooting decoy to attract wildfowl such as snipe and duck.

© Pete Johnson

The site of Pole Cottage is now an enclosure of mature hawthorn, beech and Scots pine trees providing an important wildlife habitat on the Long Mynd plateau.

This photograph, taken about 1937, shows Harry Boulton's shop in Church Stretton. As a game and poultry dealer, he provided an outlet for the surplus game shot on the Long Mynd.

Counting the Grouse

Red grouse were introduced onto the Long Mynd in the 1840s in order to improve the bag from the day's shoot which did not include grouse at the time. These game birds, flying low and for a short distance, proved particularly challenging and provided good sport. Their release on the Long Mynd has probably saved the hill from later enclosure attempts.

The red grouse population on the Long Mynd was considerably higher a century ago than it is now. Even as recently as 1975, the season's bag was as high as 113 brace but numbers declined rapidly in subsequent years. It appears to be recovering now as a result of the heather management by the National Trust described on page 27.

The National Trust, in collaboration with local wildlife groups, monitors the health of the grouse population on the Long Mynd each year. Since grouse are secretive birds and stay in the deep heather during the breeding season they are rarely seen during the daytime. Nevertheless around sunset on spring evenings, territorial males make a noisy and conspicuous display flight. Observers located at intervals along the Portway record the position of all sightings for two hours around sunset which, when collated and mapped, provides an accurate count of breeding territories for year by year comparison.

Robin Hood Butts and Shooting Butts

Two of the barrows on the Mickleburgh 1834 map near Dunkley Nap on the Long Mynd are labelled Robin Hoods Butts. The place name Robin Hood occurs throughout England and was first recorded in 1292. There are many features around the country named Robin Hoods Butts and are associated with the legendary figure who, with his men, exercised with their longbows and used the barrows as target practice. Since the advent of shooting for sport, artificial shooting butts were constructed on grouse moors which were camouflaged structures to provide shelter and cover for the shooting parties. One such was constructed on the Shooting Box barrow.

© NT Shropshire Hills

One of the largest burial mounds on the Long Mynd close to the Portway, known as the Shooting Box disc barrow, had been partially hollowed out in the early 1800s to provide shelter and cover for shooting parties. Then, in the early 1890s a concrete shelter was erected which was later replaced by a more substantial structure (above) which was subsequently demolished in 1992. There were several other shooting butts erected at strategic sites on the moor. The abundance of heather on either side of the Portway (below) provides an ideal habitat for grouse.

© Dave Laubert

Midland Gliding Club

IN AUGUST 1934 the Long Mynd became a base for gliding because of the five mile long west-facing ridge which, with a good westerly wind, would deflect the air upwards. In addition, gliding benefitted from the hill top being covered with heather which heats up rapidly in the suns rays so providing strong thermal currents. Gliding was a new sport and one which the military realised was a cheaper and faster way to train pilots than using aircraft. This resulted in the government giving £5,000 towards the establishment of the gliding station which became known as the Midland Gliding Club.

The first site was a five acre patch of grazing pasture rented from the tenant farmer but without the permission of the owner. There were already conflicts of interest between bilberry pickers and grouse shooters and having gliders take-off and land in the middle of the grouse moor at the beginning of the shooting season was an additional source of conflict.

These conflicts of interest were further heightened by the crowds who came to see the antics of these aviators. When gliding was in progress, hundreds of spectators, many with motor vehicles and dogs invaded the hill; they probably doing more harm to the grouse than the gliders did. In March 1935, the hill owner, Max Wenner, successfully obtained a court injunction to stop all glider flying. However, within a few months the gliding club negotiated a new larger site (25 acres) under a different owner further to the south which is still in use today.

Among the many visitors to the gliding station was one very famous aviatrix, Amy Johnson, who became a member. She had flown solo to Australia in 1930 in her Gypsy Moth *Jason*. Once again, her presence on the Long Mynd in 1938 drew large crowds onto the hill. Another notable club member from 1945 to 1951 was a member of the Thai royal family, Prince Birabongse.

The gliders get airborne either by using an aerotow cable attached to a tug aircraft or by a winch with a long reel of wire. When the wire gets pulled in, the glider gets the speed to fly into the air like a kite.

Long Mynd Soaring Club

The Long Mynd is one of the best westerly ridges in the UK and, with a long tradition of gliding, it has also become the home of the Long Mynd Soaring Club since 1975. The club owns the field at the top of the Long Mynd adjacent to the Gliding Club and is the launch site for paragliding and hang gliding.

Second World War

During the Second World War, all gliding operations ceased. The plateau was considered a possible landing zone for invasion and trenches were dug across the former landing field. Some local people maintain that mines were placed also which would have been unfortunate for the hill sheep. The local Home Defence force maintained a lookout on the hill. In Carding Mill Valley, units of transport motorcyclists undertook training on the valley sides while near Town Brook Hollow, live-fire training at the former rifle range continued. Live ordnance is still occasionally discovered on the hill.

The threat of fire bombs being dropped on the Long Mynd to provide beacons for German planes *en route* for South Wales led to the creation of a number of small pools, the sole purpose of which was to provide reservoirs of water that could be pumped (by stirrup hand pump) onto burning heather, a task that would have been performed by the Home Guard who kept a vigil for the enemy on the high ground.

© Beyond Extreme

The hill itself became an important landmark for both sides in the Second World War but at the same time it was a hazardous obstacle. American pilots recognized it as being near to their base at Condover aerodrome but one of their Avro Anson planes crashed-landed on Cothercott Hill, fortunately without loss of life. Three other aeroplanes are recorded as having crashed or landed on the hill during the war years. A Wellington bomber successfully put down above Haddon Hill when it was running short on fuel. The crew were saved and the aircraft was later recovered. In other incidents, an Oxford Airspeed trainer crashed into Ashes Valley killing the two pupil airmen, and the pilot died when a Spitfire crashed on the Long Mynd near Church Stretton. As yet, there are no local memorials to these airmen.

Shropshire Artillery Volunteers

The 1st Shropshire Artillery Corps was formed in 1860. In 1880 it amalgamated with the Staffordshire Artillery Volunteers to become known as the 1st Shropshire and Staffordshire Artillery Volunteers. In 1902 it became the 1st Shropshire and Staffordshire Royal Garrison Artillery (Volunteers). Finally in April 1908 it was formed into the Shropshire Royal Horse Artillery. It was initially based at the Drill Hall, Coleham, Shrewsbury, but sub-units were formed at Wellington and Church Stretton.

The Long Mynd was used for training the Volunteers in artillery practice, manoeuvres and carbine drill

Wives would often accompany Officers at camps, staying with their husbands at The Hotel in Church Stretton. Photograph about 1876.

(a short rifle carried by cavalry and the mounted artillery). The Long Mynd ranges were used only during the summer months with the guns being pulled up by teams of cart-horses, some of which were hired from the Church Stretton Posting Establishment in Burway Road. Blacksmiths were reported to have done well shoeing horses and mending broken limber chains at exorbitant prices.

The Volunteers used the railway to travel from Shrewsbury to Church Stretton. Men, horses,

food and all their equipment arrived by specially chartered trains and the band often played as they marched through the town before going up to the gun platform, the band preceding the gun teams and watched and accompanied by many townspeople. They wore navy blue uniforms, white belts and pill-box hats. Their camps brought trade to the town as well as the glamour of military bands playing in the evening outside the officers' mess in *The Hotel*. The Volunteers' Band also played at local functions such as the Church Stretton Flower Show.

About 1865 a gun platform was established on the Long Mynd to the southwest of the Devil's Mouth near Burway Road. This consisted of four brick bases on which naval-type cannons were placed overlooking Ashes Hollow with their target on Round Hill, Little Stretton. During practise, a red flag would fly from a pole nearby. Eventually, as guns become more manoeuvrable, the bases became unnecessary and were broken up.

On one occasion the Volunteer gunners missed their target and shelled Minton. Fortunately they used solid practice shot which damaged some buildings but no one was hurt.

Gunnery practice with an Armstrong breech loader.

The terrified villagers sent a horseman *post haste* to the Church Stretton police to report the matter and a police constable immediately rode up to the gun platform to tell the gunners. On another occasion in 1880, a man from Little Stretton was killed in a similar incident. Numerous cannon balls dropped into Ashes Hollow; many of these were collected by children during the Second World War to aid the campaign for iron. Some can still be found today.

The Battery was originally commanded by Col. William Field, at one time joint owner of *The Hotel*, which became the Officers' Mess during annual camps and weekend training. Officers would often be accompanied by their wives who stayed there and would visit them in the field. In the evening the regimental band, with the men in their navy blue uniforms, white belts and pill box hats, would play outside *The Hotel* for the officers and their wives who were dining inside. After the turn of the century the ranges were no longer used. Several summer camps for the Volunteers were held in fields behind Ashbrook Farm and also below Caradoc and Helmeth Hill near the present Battlefield Estate.

The King's Shropshire Light Infantry (KSLI)

WITH THE reorganization in 1908 of the Volunteers into the Territorial Volunteers for Home Defence, the demands on the Long Mynd changed. At times, the hill was used by visiting camps for manoeuvres. In 1908, the fourth Battalion of the King's Shropshire Light Infantry brought 570 men to Church Stretton and set up camp in a field on the Shrewsbury Road opposite Carding Mill Valley Road. They undertook extensive exercises on the hill, often using the ancient ditches as defensive lines. Further exercises continued in the area and on the hill throughout the Great War years and afterwards.

The KSLI marching down Sandford Avenue in 1909.

The 1st Battalion KSLI Scouts.

The 1st Battalion KSLI camp off Shrewsbury Road.

Foraging on the Long Mynd

POOR PEOPLE have always foraged in the countryside for anything that was edible or useful to supplement their diet and income. Villagers around the Long Mynd had the benefit of the common land on their doorstep and a wide choice of natural products to collect without the hindrance of trespassing on agricultural land. The historic rights of the Long Mynd commoners to the pasture allowed them to graze animals as well as to forage for fruit, flowers, fungi and foliage.

Harvesting acorn to feed swine. From the Queen Mary Psalter, *1310–1320.*

Bracken would be gathered for bedding for their cattle, acorns for the pigs, elderberries, sloes, blackberries, crab apples, mushrooms, cob nuts and chestnuts garnered for their own consumption or sale. Lapwing and curlew eggs were collected and sent to luxury-food companies. Because of its absorption capacity and slight acidity, sphagnum moss was used for wound dressings and large quantities were collected for use during the First World War.

Bilberries

The most important product of the hill, as far as the poor people were concerned, were the bilberries or, as they were called locally, wimberries. Their juice yielded an intense purple dye which was used for dyeing wool and cotton and was in great demand by the Lancashire and Yorkshire mills.

© Chris Stratton

During the height of the picking season, up to 500 people, mostly women and children, would be on the hill using special comb scoops (above) to gather the berries. They were sold to local traders or buyers from the mills for 4d–6d a quart. In 1885, it was estimated that £600–£800 was made by the local families who had picked 30,000 quarts of berries during that season. During those weeks the family could earn more than the husbands and was a significant boose to the local economy. It was said that the extra income gained by each family was enough to provide clothes and shoes for their children. The local schools had to close because most of the children were absent; an absence which continued during the subsequent blackberry season.

Bilberry picking slowly declined after the first world war possibly because more sheep were grazing on the hill and eating the young bilberry shoots. It eventually ceased in 1953 because of the national rail strike that autumn.

© Pentabus Project

Buyers of bilberries used these large baskets to transport the fruit to the northern mills.

The Rev'd Donald Carr said in 1865 'To the poor people for miles around, whinberry picking is the great event of the year. The whole family betake themselves to the hill with the early morning carrying with them the provisions for the day and not infrequently a kettle to prepare tea forms part of their heavy load. I know no more picturesque sight than that presented by the summit of the Long Mynd towards four o'clock on an August afternoon when the numerous fires are lit among the heather and as many kettles steaming away on top of them, while noisy chattering groups of women and children are clustered around, glad to rest after a hard day's work'.

Dead Men

THE LONG MYND can be dangerous place when covered by snow and especially in blizzard conditions. Such conditions are less frequent nowadays but in previous times snow would often lay on the ground obliterating every landmark for months at a time, At times like these, the Long Mynd has taken the lives of a number of travellers who have attempted to traverse its trackless plateau including two drovers who lost their lives in bad weather in 1828 near the *Thresholds*. Several places bear ominous names such as Deadman's Hollow, Devil's Mouth, Deadman's Batch and the like.

A dead man was found near Dunkley Nap near the Woolstaston boundary with Church Stretton. The Woolstaston parish refused to bury him and this was used in evidence by the people of Church Stretton in 1743 to force the boundary of the neighbouring manor off the hill and which resulted in Woolstaston losing its common land on the hill and possibly the reason for the thin wedge of Church Stretton parish to the north-west. It may be why the batch to the south-east of Dunkley Nap became known as Deadman's Batch in the upper reaches of Broad Brook.

The brook starting from Wilderley Hill was once called Dead Man's Brook, the ford that crossed it lower down was Dead Man's Ford and the lane from Picklescott to the ford was Dead Man's Lane.

An old map of Ratlinghope (1698) marks the site where a dead woman was found near the Shooting Box. The last fair of the year held at Church Stretton on Saint Andrew's day (30th November) had acquired the title of Deadman's Fair because men and women returning from it have been known to perish while endeavouring to reach their homes across the hill. At one time, the church bells of Wentnor church were rung that night to guide people home after a man lost his way and died; this was known as the dead man's peal.

A remarkable if not unprecedented experience was that which befell the Rev'd Donald Carr, the Rector of Woolstaston, who was lost in the snow on the Long Mynd for a night and a day in January, 1865. His story is told on page 164.

Netebech

The wood of Netebech extended from Church Stretton to All Stretton and centred on The Batch north of Novers Hill. In 1235 in the northern part of the wood apparently much of the oak had been felled for dread, it was alleged, of Welsh raiders lurking in it. It was thought that they had been the 57 men who a certain Richard of Minton had killed in the batch two years before and who received 57 shillings bounty for their heads.[12]

The Burway

Jonathan's Rock

JONATHAN WAS a drover who lived at Ty-nant, Islawr dref, half an hour's walk westwards from Dolgellau on the 'Old Road' that lies under the slopes of Cadair Idris. His job was driving the Welsh black cattle known as runts to Smithfield Market in London for Ifor Jones, a large landowner from nearby Bala.

In 1840, Jonathan arrived at Bala from his home to gather his herd from the Great House accompanied by his three corgi dogs and a collie. He was invited into the house to meet Mr Jones by Megan, a maid servant.

Throughout his long and arduous journey to London together with other drovers and their dogs, Jonathan's mind, when not shouting controlling commands to the convoy of cattle, was thinking of that maid servant, Megan, many miles away in Bala.

Weeks later, his cattle sold, the return journey from London began, carrying the money to deliver to Mr Jones. This walk had more purpose now and on arriving at his destination he discreetly enquired about Megan only to be told that she was no longer in service, her family having moved to All Stretton in Shropshire.

It was many months later on another return trek from the London that Jonathan made a detour from his usual route home and visited the small cottage in All Stretton where Megan lived. He stayed for over a week, spending many hours walking with her up the valley to Holly Batch and then to the 'Great Rock'. They became a familiar sight in the locality and talk of marriage was on the tongues of the villagers. Jonathan then returned to Wales to complete his business with Mr Jones.

He returned to Shropshire later in November with his few belongings and his faithful collie dog only to learn that Megan had been tragically killed by a bolting horse and trap. His heart broken, Jonathan walked up the Valley and on to the top. His body was found later in the shelter of the 'Great Rock', his life finished. Later a fitting burial was held nearby. Ever since, the valley has been called Jonathan's Batch.

© Barrie Raynor

Jonathan's Batch, with Jonathan's Rock on the skyline

The Rev'd Donald Carr's Night in the Snow

THE REV'D DONALD Carr was Rector of Woolstaston Church at the northern end of the Long Mynd. For over eight years he had also taken the afternoon service at Ratlinghope church on the west side of the Long Mynd. On Sunday the 29th January 1865, after having taken his Woolstaston morning service, he planned to take his usual four-mile trek across the Long Mynd to Ratlinghope for their afternoon service and be back at Woolstaston in time for the evening service.

The winter of 1865 was the worst during the 19th century in Shropshire. Knowing a difficult journey lay ahead, Carr skipped lunch when he set out to Ratlinghope taking with him a small flask of brandy and a servant with a horse. The sensible twelve mile road trip was impassable so they took his usual Long Mynd route which he had done hundreds of times. However, the horse soon became stuck in deep, impenetrable snowdrifts. Within a mile Carr sent the servant and horse back, continuing alone on foot. Battling through thigh-deep snow he found the only way to negotiate deeper drifts was on his hands and knees. He arrived safely in Ratlinghope in time for the service. Afterwards, he declined offers of board and lodgings for the night and began his return trip for Woolstaston's evening service.

During the afternoon the weather had deteriorated. Struggling through gale force winds, the driving snow and sleet stung his eyes frequently knocking him off his feet and disorientating him. As night fell, he grappled against the elements but suddenly he slipped, plummeting down into a ravine into the rocky valley below. He managed to stop his descent and gingerly dropped to the bottom of the ravine into 20 ft snowdrifts. He eventually clambered up the other side of the valley struggling through waist deep snow, before plummeting again into another ravine, this time losing his gloves. Icicles formed in his short beard stretching to his waist and his hair was a block of ice. Exhausted, he continued, falling into deep snow every two or three steps. As dawn broke, he realised he was snow blind. Unable to see, he fell numerous times and dropped several hundred feet down the Lightspout waterfall near Carding Mill Valley, losing his boots as he fell.

His Woolstaston parishioners had embarked on a rescue mission the night before but had been beaten back by the weather. In the morning, they searched again, reaching Ratlinghope only to learn that Carr had set off home over twelve hours earlier. When a body of another man was found in the snow nearby, the parishioners returned to Woolstaston convinced that he had perished in the snow too.

On the Monday morning with frostbitten fingers and toes, Carr heard children's voices. Scared of the ice-covered creature they saw, they ran off, telling adults about the bogeyman in Carding Mill Valley. Curious locals soon realised it was Carr and welcomed him into their homes. After some warm refreshments, he was helped to nearby Church Stretton where a horse and cart was instructed to take him home. Further snowdrifts meant that he had to abandon this at Leebotwood for the final two-mile journey home on foot.

On his way, he met a Woolstaston parishioner bound for Leebotwood's post office with letters formally announcing his death! Amazed at his survival, this man helped Carr back to Woolstaston, 27 hours after having left to make his way to Ratlinghope. He recorded his experience in the book *A Night in the Snow*.[13]

The Jack Mytton Way

J ACK MYTTON was a totally spoilt child who grew up to be a drunken wastrel but has since come to be known as one of Shropshire's more beloved eccentrics. The Jack Mytton Way is a bridleway route across South Shropshire and the Long Mynd dedicated to his memory.

His father died when he was two years of age. As heir, he subsequently inherited the family seat at Halston Hall, near Oswestry. As a young boy, Jack was sent to Westminster School but was expelled only a year after matriculation for fighting a master at the school. He was then sent to Harrow School from where he was also expelled three days later. He was subsequently educated by a series of private tutors who he tormented with practical jokes which included leaving a horse in one tutor's bedroom. Despite having achieved very little academically, Jack was granted entry to Cambridge University where he brought with him 2,000 bottles of port to sustain himself during his studies. He left Cambridge without a degree because he said he found university life boring.

Upon receiving his full inheritance he set about spending it at an unsustainable rate. He was an extremely accomplished horseman and keen hunter. Indeed it is said that he used to train his horses for hunting by riding them up and down the staircases within his home at Halston Hall. A favourite horse, Baronet, had full and free range inside the Hall and would lie in front of the fire with Jack. He indulged his enjoyment for horse racing and gambling and had some success at both. In 1826, as a result of a bet, he is said to have ridden his horse into the *Bedford Hotel*, Leamington Spa, up the grand staircase and onto the balcony from which he jumped, still seated on his horse, over the diners in the restaurant below and out through the window onto the Parade.

Another obsession was fox hunting. Jack had hunted with his own pack of hounds from the age of ten. He would go hunting in any kind of weather. His usual winter gear was a light jacket, thin shoes, linen trousers and silk stockings but in the thrill of the chase he would strip down and continue the chase naked. He is also recorded as crouching naked in snow drifts and swimming winter rivers in full spate.

He had a wardrobe consisting of 150 pairs of hunting breeches, 700 pairs of handmade hunting boots, 1,000 hats and some 3,000 shirts. He also had numerous pets in his manor, including some 2,000 dogs comprising fox hounds, pointers and retrievers; his favourites were fed on steak and champagne. Some dogs wore livery, others were costumed.

Despite him also becoming Mayor of Oswetry, High Sheriff of Shropshire and MP for Shrewsbury, contemporary society found his behaviour scandalous. Once he picked a fight with a tough Shropshire miner who disturbed his hunt and the bare knuckle fight lasted 20 rounds before the miner gave up. On another occasion, he released foxes in the *Lion Hotel,* Shrewsury.

Jack Mytton ended up in the King's Bench debtor's prison in Southwark, London. He died there in 1834 a 'round-shouldered, tottering old-young man bloated by drink, worn out by too much foolishness, too much wretchedness and too much brandy' in one report.

The Long Mynd in Literature

THE NOVELIST Rosa Mackenzie Kettle wrote a novel entitled *Carding Mill Valley* in 1882. This novel is a romance set in the Shropshire Hills. To everyone's surprise it was reprinted in 2002. The novelist Henry Kingsley wrote a novel called *Stretton* in 1869 based around the area. Other literature that uses the Long Mynd as a backdrop is the ever popular *Lone Pine* series by Malcolm Saville which is still in print and Mary Webb's *Gone to Earth* (1912), a novel based in South Shropshire and filmed by Hollywood in 1949 using location shots on the Burway. She also wrote *The Golden Arrow* which makes reference to the 'signposts which rose from various lost points in the vast expanse, shepherds' signposts pointing vaguely down vague ways'.

Sheena Porter's book *The Knockers* draws on the history and folklore of the Long Mynd and is entwined with a contemporary story of children trying

Mary Webb

to solve the mystery of eerie knocking sounds sometimes heard on the Long Mynd.

Pearce's Tea rooms in Carding Mill Valley promoted their business as the 'Country of Mary Webb'. Mary Webb's novel *Precious Bane* serves as the basis for the parody by Stella Gibbons in *Cold Comfort Farm*.

The Long Mynd upland formed part of Housman's *Blue Remembered Hills* and it is known that in 1899 he stayed in Church Stretton at *The Hotel*. As already noted (page 152), Ronald Stevens also wrote several books about his experiences as a falconer on the Long Mynd.

Malcolm Saville

© Malcolm Saville Society

ALTHOUGH born and raised in Sussex, Malcolm Saville (1901–1982) has always been closely associated with this area of Shropshire, following the success of his series of *Lone Pine* stories which were set on and around the Long Mynd and the Stiperstones. The books were published between 1943 and 1978 and over a million copies sold.

The Saville family first visited South Shropshire in 1936 and Malcolm was very taken with the area. When war came the family was evacuated to Cwm Head at the southern end of the Long Mynd. His first children's book, *Mystery at Witchend*, is a thrilling story of German spies in the Shropshire hills. Nineteen further titles followed in the *Lone Pine* series and he wrote over ninety books (both fiction and non-fiction) in his career. Although many of his books are now out of print, his influence still brings many visitors to the area to see the sights and to relive their childhood memories.

The attraction of Malcolm Saville's books, as opposed to those by his more famous contemporary Enid Blyton, was that he set his stories in real places and encouraged his readers to come and explore them for themselves. With the detailed description of the countryside, the wildlife and the atmosphere, the reader can almost feel the wind blowing in the trees, hear the sound of the ravens and feel the warmth of the sun or the cold chill of the Long Mynd mist. He had the ability to immerse the reader right into the story and place as if really there.

Malcolm was a deeply religious man. This comes through in his books with the deep sense of loyalty between the various characters, Their constant struggle to fight evil or injustice is cleverly woven into the story. He uses his personal beliefs and his deep love of the countryside as a base line without forcing his views onto the reader, so that the reader has to find those hidden depths for himself.

© Malcolm Saville Society

Dr Mott's Road is an old track, now a bridleway that leads from the head of Carding Mill Valley onto the top of Long Mynd. It was the route used by the Dr Charles Mott, who had a medical practice in Church Stretton from about 1819 to 1863, to reach his patients on the other side of the Long Mynd. His route on horse-back took him through Carding Mill Valley, up a rough track over the Long Mynd, across the Port Way and down another track to Ratlinghope. He was a well-liked member of the community and this track was improved by public subscription in 1850 so that he could use it more easily.

Buxton quarry, All Stretton. Inset photo: the quartz veins which characterise Buxton rock.

Quarries and Mines

THE SHALY ROCKS of the Long Mynd have not been used much as a building material. In general, they make poor building stone and have been quarried only to a small extent, initially only by the commoners by right or custom and few quarries were ever in commercial production. As with all the different rocks which compose the Long Mynd, their layers (strata) can usually be traced in a north-eastern to south-westerly trend along the length of the hill.

Buxton rock is the name given to one of the lower layers of rock forming the Long Mynd. It is a layer varying from 3 m to 7 m thick and is at its thickest at Buxton quarry near the mouth of The Batch in All Stretton. The same layer appears near the mouth of most of the valleys on the east side of the Long Mynd.

This stratum of Buxton rock resulted from ash ejected into the air from an enormous erupting volcano around 565 million years ago and descended onto the surface of the sea before sinking and forming a layer of mud and subsequently being compressed to the rock we see today. A feature of this rock is the number of white veins scattered throughout. These are small cracks which have been filled with the mineral quartz which had crystallised from very hot silica-laden water forced up from deep below the earth's surface. Buxton quarry is the largest and most important on the Long Mynd.

Because it is the hardest of the Buxton rock (in contrast the very thick layer of soft shale beneath), it had some use as a building material and as road stone and was used in the construction in 1902 of St Michael's Church, All Stretton. Material from the quarry is used by the National Trust to repair paths on the Long Mynd.

The name Buxton is derived from Buckstone, the field name recorded on the 1838 tithe award map given to a field to the north of and adjacent to the quarry. The field name may be so called because 'buck stone' is also a common medieval name for a place where there is a large isolated rock possibly associated with deer.

The huge quarry at Bayston Hill produces a very high quality road stone which maintains its irregular edges well and thereby helps to provide good vehicle traction. It comes from a higher (and later) stratum from the same rock formation which is found near Pole Bank. That the same rock is present at both sites shows that the rock formations of the Long Mynd disappear below the surface and appear again further north at Bayston Hill and, incidentally, again north of Shrewsbury.

Coal

One of the smaller Shropshire coalfields occurs around Leebotwood and lies above the now-submerged Long Mynd rock formations. The Leebotwood colliery operated only from 1784 to about 1875. It covered 41 acres (16.6 ha) and had four shallow pits 30–60 m deep, the main colliery being at New House Farm (GR 482999), 700 m north of Leebotwood. The coal was used for making lime, bricks and tiles on the site. Old maps give clues to the presence of coal elsewhere in the vicinity with names such as Old Colliery, Coalpit field and Pitchford.

Mining

Rocks on the northern slopes of the Long Mynd around Pulverbatch and south to Cothercott Hill contain extensive mineral veins, particularly barytes ($BaSO_4$), that were widely exploited up to the 1950s. Much thinner veins of barytes were possibly mined near Hill End Farm at the southern end of the Long Mynd, There is some evidence for small scale workings for copper on the western slopes of the hill. These veins are part of the much larger area of materialization to the west of the Stiperstones which was of huge national economic importance from Roman times through to the mid 20th century.

© Peter Toghill

The barytes vein, about 12 inches thick, at the entrance to Cothercott mine.

Managing the Landscape

M AN-INDUCED change has been taking place on the Long Mynd since the arrival of the first hunter-gatherers some time after the last ice age 10,000 years ago. Such change is likely to continue into the future, perhaps more so as pressures from an increased population and changes to the climate become progressively more intense. Extensive management work is constantly required to maintain the wonderful views and the flora and fauna associated with the heath land that we have now.

The question is - manage for what? If nothing were done, then sheep numbers would change, heather, gorse and bracken would grow uncontrolled, streams may get blocked and possibly overflow, paths may deteriorate and dense scrubby woodland could eventually take over. Doing nothing is therefore not an option.

The aim of the National Trust is to restore the heath land by improving the condition of the heather, to control the bracken and provide a variety of quality wetland and grassland so as to provide the optimum habitat for as many species of birds, mammals, amphibians, invertebrates, lichens, mosses and flowers as possible.

Management is also directed towards providing small-scale diversity by breaking up monocultures, increasing the number of pools and wetland flushes, clearing bracken from the plateau but not from near flushes or from the hillsides, maintain short grass by monitoring any overgrazing and maintain the scattered trees on the hillsides.

Regeneration around New Pool Reservoir.
Downy birch, grey willow, rowan, hawthorn, dog rose and bramble are now well established with secondary oak and alder emerging. This photo shows how trees and shrubs have naturally established themselves since 1978 in the sheltered valley floor provided the sheep are fenced out. This compares with the heather which has naturally returned on the plateau (upper photo) where sheep have been removed from the land on the right hand side of the fence.

Although the National Trust owns only about half of the hill, surrounding landowners and other bodies are involved in complementary work to improve the habitat of the remainder of the Long Mynd.

In any case, the landscape will inevitably evolve as a result of environmental influences such as changes in the climate as well as natural vegetation succession.

New Zealand Pygmyweed

New Zealand Pygmyweed is a very invasive non-native pond weed which smothers all other plant-life and is notoriously difficult to get rid off. This perennial herb grows submerged in sheltered waters up to three metres deep or on damp ground. It can grow vigorously at the expense of the indigenous plant species with adverse effects on aquatic ecosystems through light limitation, oxygen depletion and changes in pH.

Fortunately it has only been found in a single pond on the golf course on the Long Mynd. It was removed by clearing the pond (and its 300 golf balls!), chemically spraying it to destroy the remaining weed and then lining the pool with black plastic to try to prevent its re-growth.

Himalayan Balsam

Himalayan balsam is rampant on Castle Hill smothering everything under it. It is an impressive plant that can grow to over 3 m tall. The large flowers are attractive and range through many shades of pink and are big enough to hide a foraging bumble bee.

© Barrie Raynor

Himalayan balsam.

Scree

Weathering and erosion by frost action over many centuries has resulted in an accumulation of rocky debris on some valley sides, particularly on the east facing slope of Townbrook Valley (photo below). The scree consists of fragments of very variable size. The small pockets of soil which accumulate between the rocks support species such as heather, gorse, bilberry and foxglove together with a variety of bryophytes and lichens. The isolation from grazing produces an interesting fern community. A combination of factors, such as the high rainfall, the abundance of deep, humid crevices, the freedom from grazing and plant competition and the ease with which spores can settle and establish serve to suit this sensitive group of plants. The biggest threat to this habitat is the inadvertent dislodging material by walkers and sheep which can damage the vulnerable vegetation.

© Barrie Raynor

Slope Failure

In 2001 after a prolonged period of high rainfall the stream in Carding Mill Valley extended its meander to undercut the slope of Haddon Hill destroying the footpath and causing slope failure. Because water speeds up on the outside of the bend, it improves its ability to both pick up and transport material from the base of the slope and soon caused the landslip shown (photo). Rock material of varying size was transported downstream and the heavier material deposited at the inside of the next meander where the water velocity is reduced.

In order to stabilise the slope and prevent further erosion, cages of stones (gabions) have been placed at the foot of the slope which eventually provided a site for vegetation to re-establish. One of these gabions subsequently failed because it was itself undermined by the stream and spilt its contents. This site graphically illustrates the process of natural erosion and deposition of material by a stream which over centuries straightens and widens the valley.

Footpath Repair

Repair to the bridleways, especially the Portway and Dr Mott's Road, have been carried out by the National Trust using stone airlifted in by helicopter from the Bayston Hill quarry where the same Long Mynd rock re-emerges.

Erosion also occurs on popular footpaths. When footpaths are reduced to soil, they become soft and boggy; people will always take the easiest and driest route, so they will walk around boggy patches if possible and thereby widen the footpaths. Paths also get deeper as each layer of soil disappears; this is a big problem on slopes when it rains as water follows the easiest route downhill, runs into the indentation of a footpath and through 'gullying' increases the erosion of the path. To alleviate this, drainage channels (wumps) are cut about every ten metres across most paths (more frequently on steep paths) and can significantly reduce erosion from run-off but they do need regular clearing.

Woodland Management

Woodland and dense scrub are not a major habitat on the Long Mynd and are not of high conservation value, although they do provide additional habitat diversity. The larches have been clear felled at Handless Bank and heather and bilberry have successfully regenerated as a result. Forestry Commission land at the southern end of the Long Mynd should ideally be felled in a similar manner so that it can revert to heath and provide proper biodiversity.

At The Wern (right) between Callow Hollow and Minton Small Batch there was a mixed wood containing mature broad-leafed trees, poplars and conifers. The poplars and conifers have been felled and there has been some replanting with young native broad-leafed trees.

Most of the large numbers of hawthorns in all the batches are getting very old; they are being replaced by natural regeneration and planting of young specimens grown from a seed bank. It is necessary for grazing levels to be kept sufficiently high to prevent dense scrub from forming.

The Wern during the clearance of conifers.

© NT Shropshire Hills

Rabbits

RABBITS WERE introduced into Britain in the 11th century by Norman settlers who established them as semi-domestic livestock. All our modern wild rabbits are descended from Norman rabbits who escaped and survived in the wild. Rabbits were kept for their meat and fur, the meat being considered a delicacy and therefore was consumed primarily by the upper classes. At this time the adult rabbit was known as a coney and the word rabbit referred to the young of the species.

A 13th century warren.

The Normans kept their coneys in enclosures and allowed them to breed freely, then culled the younger rabbits for food. These enclosures were called coneygarths and were usually surrounded by a stone wall to keep the animals in. It seems that medieval rabbits were less keen on excavating than their modern counterparts! Warrens were constructed for them on light free-draining soils and pipes and artificial burrows were installed to encourage them to breed, a necessity that seems laughable today. These artificial mounds could be of considerable size ranging from less than six metres up to 150 m in length.

The Normans used ferrets and nets to capture the coneys when they wanted them and a Norman lord would employ warreners whose job it was to ensure the health and size of the warren and to provide the required number for meat on demand.

Lords of the manors had to apply to the king to get a 'grant of free warren'. This was not always given, particularly in the case of the Long Mynd which was part of the Royal Forest. Even at the beginning of the twentieth century, if the lord of the manor wanted to make a rabbit burrow on the common land, the commoners had no automatic right to destroy the rabbits or the burrows. However, just as the lord could bring action against a commoner for putting too many beasts on the common, so a commoner could bring action against the lord if he thought the rabbits were increasing in numbers and destroying his pasturage.

On the Long Mynd

Medieval warrens are evident to the south of Black Knoll where the names Rabbit Warren and Warren House are marked on OS maps. There were also warrens at the top of Rectory Field called Far Cunnery and Near Cunnery on the land between the *Longmynd Hotel* and Tiger Hall in Church Stretton which was part of the glebe of the Rector and which gave rise to the name of Cunnery Road nearby. The road called Trevor Hill in Church Stretton was originally called Rabbit Burrow.

Rabbits are abundant on upper south-facing slopes of many of the valleys where there is plenty of gorse and bracken cover. In Carding Mill Valley on the south-facing slopes of Haddon Hill there are many shallow burrows. The rabbits are active at dawn and dusk, hiding during the day under the canopy of nearby gorse or bracken to avoid the ever present buzzard searching for a meal.

© Northeastwildlife.co.uk

Church Stretton Golf Club

The Golf Club House in 1905. It was built in 1899.

THIS IS THE oldest 18-hole golf course in Shropshire. It was laid out and opened in 1898 to a design by James Braid, a well known golf course designer. It was originally of 9 holes but was extended to 18 holes in 1903 and is now just over 5,000 yards in length. The course lay on land owned by the Church Stretton Land Co. Ltd and the lord of the manor, Ralph Beaumont Benson, but over which the Long Mynd Commoners had grazing rights. The club owns the first fairway and the 18th hole and the National Trust owns the remainder of the course over which commoners still have grazing rights.

It is the third highest golf course in Britain and lies on the lower slopes of the Long Mynd, its height varying between 800 and 1,160 ft above sea level. The highest point is the 14th green at 1,160 ft. Because of its height, it is often covered with snow; indeed, fifty years ago when there was much more snow on the hill, the club was known as the '6-month club'.

The Long Mynd as a Teaching Resource

THE LONG MYND, and especially the Carding Mill Valley, provides an ideal opportunity for school children and students to explore and see a range of scientific principles put into practice under the guidance of experienced instructors. National Trust Education staff provide a range of courses and teaching opportunities in the valley for schools.

For many students the experience of visiting and walking in the valley is a novelty, whilst for everybody there is the opportunity for real field work which consolidates their classroom studies. Students are able to look at how land is used, study the life of a river, appreciate visitor pressures, learn about the shaping of the landscape from the archaeological and geographical evidence, as well as studying issues of citizenship such as the impact of their lifestyle on the environment, sustainability and keeping healthy.

Students learn how to help conserve the countryside by writing about litter, dams, bank breakdown, stone throwing, off-path disturbance, single file walking, dogs, bikers and the picking of flowers.

The Long Mynd needs to be maintained and students are shown the importance of footpath repairs, scree cages, tree planting, drainage traps and litter collection. They learn also the problems associated with sheep, sheep scrapes, bracken, fires and terracing (soil creep).

The valley provides a unique opportunity to examine the formation of the hills resulting from the eruptions of nearby volcanoes, examine strata, conduct tests on metamorphic, igneous and sedimentary rocks and examine stream bedload for evidence of erosion.

© Peter Carty

River Study.

By measuring the widths of the valley, the size of channel and water surface, and measuring the stream velocity, students are able to draw conclusions about the changes between upper and lower river sites.

© Yvonne Beaumont

© Chris Stratton

Field Study Laboratory.

There is a laboratory that seats 36 students who use hand lens and microscopes to examine what they have caught in the stream. Besides learning how to use a microscope, students study water pollution, identify the water invertebrates they have caught, learn their scientific names and draw the creature.

© Peter Carty

© Chris Stratton

© Chris Stratton

© Chris Stratton

© Chris Stratton

© Chris Stratton

Pond Dipping.

Specimens caught in the stream or pond are identified and inspected with hand lens or microscope in the laboratory.

© Chris Stratton

© Peter Carty

Natural History and Habitats.

The fieldwork enables students to use a range of scientific methods in their investigations by looking, for example, at what is living and growing at differing levels in the soil, in leaf litter, on the soil surface, shrub layer, on stems and bark, in the canopy and in the air, as well as comparing pond life with stream life. They learn to classify the creatures they have found as herbivores, carnivores or detritivores and develop a food chain.

© Chris Stratton

© Chris Stratton

Map and Compass.

After beginning with a variety of map reading activities including grid referencing,using a compass, learning about map symbols and orientation, students go outside to test their skills at orienteering.

© Barrie Raynor

© Paul Miller

The YHA bunkhouse in The Batch
was opened in 2006 by
Pete Postlethwaite (inset).

© Yvonne Beaumont

The hunt near Plush Hill.

A Year on the Long Mynd

THE COLOURFUL Long Mynd with its varied wildlife is a wonderful place to visit at any time of the year. In the natural world plants and animals work to different time scales and the seasonal changes which are important for the local wildlife cannot be precisely defined on the calendar. The British weather is so variable that in some years spring seems to start as early as February and autumn can go on through to the end of November. Every year is different. The following pages give a flavour of what the Long Mynd looks like each month in a typical year and what is happening on the hill.

© Richard Warren

Townbrook Valley

January

WINTER has truly come and most birds have deserted the hills, particularly if conditions are hard and snow lies on the ground for long periods. Life continues, albeit often unseen, especially if the hill is blanketed by snow.

Most invertebrates are inactive in the winter, either as adults or as larvae lying dormant under the soil or leaf litter. Some, like the golden-ringed dragonfly, survive as larvae in mud on the bottom of ponds whilst others, such as peacock butterflies lie dormant in crevices behind the bark of trees and grayling caterpillars overwinter in tussocks of grass.

On many holly trees there are little yellow blotches on the upper side of the older leaves. Inside the blotches lives the tiny grub of the holly leaf miner tunnelling away. Its parent is a small fly that laid an egg there.

Those invertebrates that do not over-winter as adults or larvae spend the winter as eggs or pupae waiting for the warmer weather before they emerge.

This can be the harshest time for birds as food supplies become scarcer. If the weather in Scandinavia is severe flocks of redwing and fieldfares come to Britain and are often seen in valleys where there are trees with berries such as rowan and hawthorn. They can be heard calling to one another with a distinctive metallic *chack* noise or a high pitched whistle.

Winter is the time for foxes to start mating; the dog fox makes short dry barks as he moves around at night. It is the vixen that makes the blood-curdling screams that are so eery on a frosty night.

Other animals are stirring too. Male grey squirrels can be seen chasing the females with two or three joining in the pursuit. They go round and round the trunks and along the branches with much excited chatter and daring leaps from tree to tree.

If there is no snow or frost, one bird that can sometimes be seen in large numbers is the golden plover, flocks of which may congregate near High Park feeding on invertebrates in the short wet vegetation. When they rise in the evening, they make shrill *peeoo* calls as they wheel and turn before settling down to roost at night.

Throughout the winter months, the National Trust is busy with woodland and hedge maintenance, planting trees such as hawthorn, rowan and oak on hillsides and valleys, some of which have been donated *in memoriam*. It is a good time to plant and repair hedges with hawthorn, hazel and blackthorn.

February

THIS MONTH can be as harsh as any with snow and freezing winds. However it is possible to spot hints of better things to come. Although spring is still several weeks away the first signs are there to see. Hazel catkins start to expand into golden tassels ready to release their pollen to the wind. The female part of the hazel consists of a tiny sticky tuft of red stigmas to catch the wind-borne pollen.

The first shoots of the spring bulbs are likely to be emerging. In addition, it is heartening to see the delicate snowdrops even showing through the snow. The first green shoots of bluebells start to appear in Rectory Wood as well as sprigs of dog's mercury under the trees.

The most striking change on the Long Mynd in winter is seen when the bracken dies down to give the hillsides their rich golden-brown colour. Bilberry loses its leaves to become green spikes, revealing a remarkable assortment of pale green lichens elaborately branched or with red tipped spikes.

Each winter the National Trust inspect the ponds on the plateau and some need clearing because they have got so overgrown with pond weed.

This month, badgers start to spring-clean their setts, clearing out the old bracken and leaves and replacing it with fresh bedding ready for the cubs which are born this month, though these do not appear above ground until April or May.

The lengthening hours of daylight prompts blackbirds to start singing again. With their leisurely fluting notes, the male guards his territory hoping to attract a mate. Robins, too, can be heard singing their winter song from high vantage points in the depths of winter as they defend their territories from intruders.

*Snowdrops arrive
Like a rumour of Spring
A paler precursor
Of 'Wonderful things'.*

*Great aunts with hankies
They whisper in white
That once they were bluebells
Who danced through the night.*

*Flowering snowdrifts
By yew-tended graves;
Reminders of chapels
Where love was displayed;
Snowdrops have sprung from the
   unyielding earth
Like manna dispensed from a
   crusader's purse.*

Richard Bonfield

March

SPRING often appears to start late on the Long Mynd. European gorse scattered at low density across parts of the hill is one of the first obvious plants to flower and can fill the air with the smell of coconut. The much more abundant western gorse, which dominates many valley sides, flowers much later in the year.

© Hilary Chambers

© Northeastwildlife.co.uk

By now, frogs are mating with vigour, having risen from the pond bottom where they spent the winter. The amorous males cling in large numbers onto the females almost suffocating her; it is surprising that the females can survive. They are all trying to ensure that all the eggs laid are fertilised. The adults stay in the pond until the weather is warmer in April.

Chiffchaffs and other breeding birds begin to arrive back in increasing numbers from mid March onwards and start singing and displaying to establish their territories. One of the first to arrive is the wheatear and they can be seen feeding among the sheep on the cropped grass.

In the hedgerows towards the end of the month the blackthorn is in flower. These small trees are covered in clouds of white blossom borne on its dark, thorn-laden branches. This shrub is sometimes confused with hawthorn but the hawthorn does not flower until May and comes into leaf before the blossom opens.

At this time queen bees are a welcome sight. On the Long Mynd, these include the bilberry bumble bee which may be seen in good numbers gathering nectar on willow by the reservoir in New Pool Hollow.

This month the National Trust surveys the condition and the flowering levels of the heather in order to assess the impact of grazing on the heathland.

© GanMed 64

One of the first of the large insects to be seen in early spring is the hairy fox moth caterpillar, often seen basking in the sun on path-sides, preparing to pupate.

The pussy willow (sallow), which is so synonymous with spring, can be seen with its bursting catkins, particularly in wet areas. The catkins are male pollen-bearing flowers which offer up their pollen to the wind to seek out female flowers. The pussy willow is usually the name given to the goat willow.

April

APRIL IS a fabulous month for wildlife as the trees and shrubs burst into leaf with fresh, vibrant green foliage. The fragile leaves are vulnerable to insect attack but this early growth is still beautiful perfection.

This month the tiny white flowers of spring annuals such as upright chickweed and shepherd's cress start to appear on the south facing dry slopes along with a host of other small plants.

In the woodland, the floor can be a mass of white wood anemone and wood garlic flowers, It is possible to catch their heady scent even before reaching them. These woodland flowers need to be pollinated and catch the available light to grow before the darkness of the filling treetop canopy envelops them. This is why they grow so early and then slowly die back in summer.

Small groups of non-breeding ravens will be feeding on the plateau and mature pairs can be seen twisting and turning in their acrobatic display flight prior to mating. Eggs are laid early and there will be young in the nest from mid March onwards. Parents may be seen foraging for food on the hillside or plateau, particularly as the young start to fledge and need increasing amounts of food during the month.

The commoners are obliged to limit the numbers of sheep and ponies on the Long Mynd. These are checked by the National Trust so that overgrazing is prevented. The ponies are rounded up by their owner, their health checked and some sold so that the numbers of mares are reduced to the agreed limit of thirty. The one or two stallions are changed every three years to prevent inbreeding.

On warm sunny days in late April slow worms and common lizards bask in the sun struggling to absorb sufficient solar radiation to become active. Palmate newts appear in many of the ponds to court and lay their eggs.

The emperor moths, which have spent the winter as pupae, emerge and on sunny days can be seen zig-zagging over heather or bilberry in search of a mate. These impressive moths will remain until late May. By the end of the month green hairstreak butterflies can also be seen around the gorse bushes on the valley sides and St Mark's flies appear in swarms, drifting over vegetation with their long legs dangling. They are a welcome food source for newly arrived migrant birds as well as residents. On the dry tracks tawny mining bees excavate burrows leaving small tell-tale pyramids of earth beside them.

April is the month when the annual red grouse count starts. Large numbers of volunteers line the Portway just before sunset over several weeks to count the male grouse who are all doing their territorial display flight.

The hillsides are now alive with lambs and the sound of their bleating and that of their mothers as they try to keep in touch with each other. For centuries sheep and their wool were the mainstay of the economy of Church Stretton and other local villages.

May

B Y MID MAY dragon and damselflies have started to emerge and quickly go about breeding. The adult damselflies bind themselves together whilst the eggs are laid on submerged plant leaves. Some dragonflies are fiercely territorial and you can often witness spectacular aerial clashes between one male and another. However they need to take care as hobbys are becoming more common on the Long Mynd and with their super-fast flight can easily hunt down these impressive insects.

All of the birds are now nesting. The stonechat, for example, nests in the heather on the steep sides of the upper valleys near bracken and gorse so that they can get food from more than one source.

The important mayfly group of insects also emerge in May, as their name suggests. The short-lived adult mayfly emerges only to mate and then die within 24 hours. The nymph stage lives for a year and needs clean water. They are an important food source for many fish are a good biological indicator of a clean environment.

This month, around disturbed ground and old sheep feeding sites, the ground can turn blood-red with the flowers of sheep's sorrel. The old name for this is sour dock or vinegar dock and its scientific name *Rumex acetosella*, indicates the presence of acetic acid or vinegar. Tasting a few leaves is refreshing on a hot day and it adds spice to salads.

In wet hollows the fly-catching sundews shine like red pearls. Their sticky hairs are to catch insects; once caught, the plant digests them to make up for the low nutrients in the soil, especially nitrogen.

During the year many of the footpath signposts and markers get knocked over by sheep and ponies rubbing up against them and these need to be re-seated. The vegetation on the sides of many of the paths starts to get overgrown and has to be strimmed back by National Trust staff.

As the days warm up, many more butterflies and moths start to appear. Orange tips may be seen egg-laying on the lady's smock in the wet flushes and the first brood of the small coppers can be seen in sunny sheltered areas. By late spring, small heath butterflies can be seen as well as many moths including the large fox moths and oak eggars.

June

THIS IS the time of year when the wildlife on Long Mynd is at its best and busiest and the insects are most active. On warm days throughout the summer, the pools are alive with the whirring of dragonfly wings. Over fifteen species can be seen including good numbers of black darters and common hawkers, typical of such upland pools.

Walking through the bracken disturbs brown silver-line moths which fly up. On the bracken fronds the brown and yellow stripy broom moth caterpillars can be seen feeding.

Every few months National Trust volunteers walk the footpaths, making repairs as necessary, clearing drainage channels and ditches. The same is true for the board walks which are checked for ant damage or deterioration. Twice a year, the stone trap at the foot of the Carding Mill Valley is cleared of the hundreds of tons of stone that has been washed down the streams. This is returned to the plateau and used to repair footpaths and bridleways.

House martins are busy catching insects on the wing to feed their young in their large cup-like mud nests under the eaves of houses and buildings in Carding Mill Valley. They can be easily distinguished from swifts by their white bellies and stubbier bodies.

In early summer, the waxy bell-like flowers of the bilberry appear providing a welcome source of nectar for the bees and other insects. The first flowering of the foxgloves appear on rocky slopes but only where the soil is slightly acidic. As the summer progresses the open flowers climb the stem of this biennial until only a few remain at the top of a tall spike.

In the wet boggy areas the distinctive tufts of cotton-like seed heads on the cotton grass as well as the pink flowers of bog pimpernel, the yellow bog asphodel and also two insect-eating plants, butterwort and sundew, can readily be found. The former was used to curdle butter presumably because it is one of the few plants to contain fat, whilst the latter was voted the county flower for Shropshire by Plantlife International members. Throughout the summer the stream sides are lined with lemon scented fern and delicate lady fern.

The breeding birds are most active at this time. Most of the birds are summer visitors, arriving between mid March and early May and leaving again during August and September. This is the best time for the National Trust to survey and count the breeding upland birds.

Snipe are the most secretive of all the birds on the Long Mynd. They are found within or close to the flushes and pools on Wildmoor. They feed in the soft ground and mud using their long bill to probe for worms and snails. Snipe are much more likely to be heard than seen; their drumming flight at dusk carries a long distance.

July

T HE FIRST of the summer migrants to depart are the cuckoos. The adults leave in July to be followed by their offspring later in the year; somehow the young find their way to Africa independently.

This month is a good time for the National Trust to assess the condition of the botanically important wet flushes which contribute so much to the wide range of habitats on the Long Mynd.

From July onwards after the birds have finished nesting and, depending on the weather, bracken cutting starts. A forage harvester cuts as much as possible and the cut bracken is taken to a nearby farm to a special composter. If the bracken were not cut annually it would become too thick and spread over former areas of grass and where flowers proliferated.

House martins and swallows are flying around at breakneck speed in pursuit of aerial prey. These opportunists twist and spin in the air and successfully catch such insects as flies and daddy long legs. They chat amongst themselves in mid air. Both may still have young in their mud nests under eaves but they eventually are encouraged to leave by the adults who swoop and chatter around them.

Later in the month large flocks of mistle thrush move up the valleys feeding on the bilberry but otherwise this a quiet time for birds and few are seen or heard. Most are preparing for their migration either to the lowlands and coasts or to Iberia and Africa. The adults moult and the newly-fledged young feed and stay hidden in the dense foliage to build up the resources for their forthcoming ordeal.

The flautist with the golden beak
Who lulls you off to lovely sleep
Is singing in a nearby tree
And when you're tucked up - safe and sound
His melody drifts all around
A song that pours from Summer earth
Like pennies from a velvet purse
As - all around our sunset town
The blackbirds bring the curtain down.

Richard Bonfield

August

THE VIBRANT summer colours of many adult insects, particularly dragonflies, darken or fade as the season progresses, although they remain active well into September. However, the second brood of small copper and wall butterflies still look fresh as they bask in the September sun on the track sides. Many moth caterpillars such as those of the fox moth continue to feed and bask in the last sunny days of summer as they prepare to overwinter. Social wasps, such as the common wasp, live in large colonies for most of the year. However, in the autumn the social structure of the nest breaks down and wasps become very noticeable around picnic sites where they search for sugary foods.

Heather is flowering at its best this month and huge swathes of it cover the plateau. It is the home of the grouse whose chicks have now grown up and are fending for themselves. From the mid-nineteenth century, the Long Mynd was managed as a grouse moor and the 12th of August, 'the glorious twelfth', was the start of the shooting season. Since shooting was stopped in 1990, careful management by the National Trust has resulted in a steady increase in grouse numbers.

© Paul Sullivan

Blackberries and bilberries are now ripe together with other berries such as hawthorn (haws), sloes and rose hips. These will provide sustenance for many birds through the harsh winter months. For now, food is plentiful although the dry ground can cause problems for the ground feeding birds.

Hot days also bring the restful sound of grasshoppers calling (stridulating) from the long grass, advertising their territories. They are difficult to spot due to their green or brown colour but soon jump to reveal themselves if disturbed, only to disappear again. Here, the species most likely to be spotted are the common green, common field and the meadow grasshopper.

© NT Shropshire Hills

Throughout the autumn the vibrant golden flowers of western gorse cover many of the valley sides and along the tracks the yellow flowers of autumn hawkbit can be seen. Bilberries provide a meal for small mammals and human visitors alike while the heather is at its best. The bracken is starting to turn a distinctive rusty brown as it dies back.

September

© Keith Laverack

THIS IS the month of the autumn equinox, a marker that highlights the changing seasons. It sees the departure of the majority of swifts. Their short stay in Britain reminds us just how fleeting summer can be. House martins and swallows are thinking about migrating and can often be seen in large numbers perched on telephone lines. Most migrant birds are, however, with us for a while yet.

© Thomas Kohler

The hedgerows are now full of ripening berries with hawthorn haws and rose hips shining red, while sloes, blackberries and elderberries are midnight black. To get to the hazel nuts you will have to race the squirrels and jays who hoard them for the winter by burying them in the ground. It is said that many oaks, particularly, are derived from such forgotten stashes.

Autumn brings great changes. Many plants die back to their storage roots below ground, overwinter as seeds or remain as a shadow of their former self above ground. The leaves of deciduous trees turn to beautiful gold, orange and red colours. They tenaciously hold them until they drop.

Animals fatten up for their winter hibernation, insect numbers decline massively as adults of many species die to leave the caterpillars or pupae to survive the winter. Certain insects are, however, noticeable at this time of year. Around the time of the harvest in August onwards the craneflies (daddy long legs) appear in their greatest numbers and seemingly fly in a haphazard rather inebriated way. The craneflies' legs break off easily as a way of escaping predators. The larval stage of this family of insects are known as leatherjackets. It is a destructive maggot-like larva which feeds on cereal and other roots but which is an important food source for many birds on the Long Mynd.

On the Long Mynd autumn is heralded by the arrival of large flocks of birds that come to Britain for the winter, such as redwing and fieldfare and later brambling and golden plover. Other birds are migrating and pass through between mid August and mid October; there appears to be more now than pass through in the spring. This is probably because birds flying north to get to their breeding grounds travel much more directly and only stop over to feed. The return migration in the autumn now includes all the new young birds. It is more leisurely and food is available in many more places.

© Barrie Raynor

In the bases of many hedges lords and ladies have totally died down other than the ripening fruiting stem, with its poisonous red berries. This is the 'lady' part.

Autumn's pincushion,
The lovely moon-pig
Is teasingly, carelessly studded
With dead September leaves
As she shuffles down the catwalk
In an off-the-hedgerow number,
Her body liberally sequinned
With hundreds of glittering fleas.

Richard Bonfield

October

© Yvonne Beaumont

I N LATE autumn the short grass on the hill can be spectacularly colourful, scattered with the crimson, orange, yellow, white or pink caps of the waxcap fungi as well as the slender golden spindle and black earth tongue fungi. One interesting species to look out for on the grassy paths amongst the heather is the scarlet caterpillar fungus. Magic mushrooms are found throughout the short grasslands and edible parasol and field mushrooms are common, particularly close to boundaries of enclosed pasture.

What appears at this time of year above ground is the spore-bearing part of the fungus, this being only a small part of the organism. Under the ground, where many grow, there are metres and metres of tiny filaments, known as hyphae, which reach out into surrounding organic matter which the fungus 'digests' as its food source. They require the wet conditions of autumn to be able to thrive. Fungi play a hugely important role in breaking down organic material such as dead leaf litter and dead animals. They are nature's recyclers, without them there would be mountains of the stuff! They also form very intimate links with the roots of all plants helping the plants access nutrients and for which in turn the fungus gets a place to grow and thrive.

Around mid October toads go into hibernation, finding logs or stones to hide beneath until spring arrives once more. Frogs also begin to hibernate at this time of the year at the bottom of ponds or some other sheltered place, ready to emerge again in the following spring.

The health of the streams on the Long Mynd is monitored now by surveying the invertebrate populations which are a sensitive measure of a stream's purity.

© Northeastwildlife.co.uk

Photos opposite: The top four are typical woodland fungi and the lower four typical grassland fungi.

© Northeastwildlife.co.uk

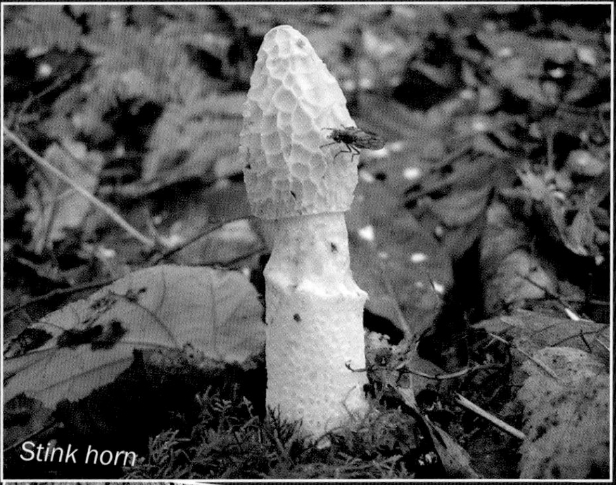

Stink horn

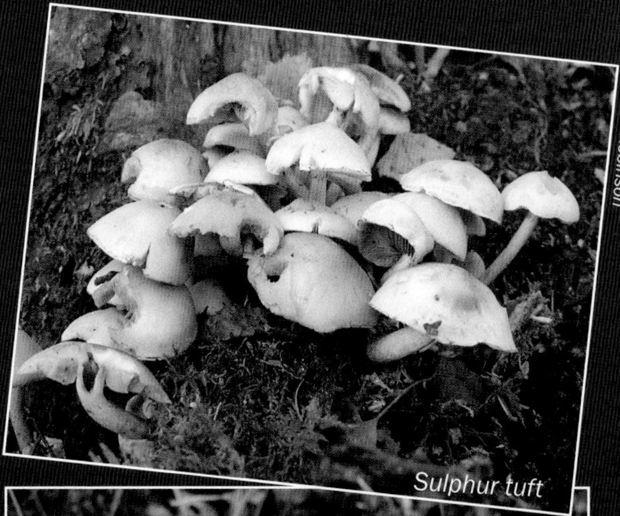

© Nick Robinson

Sulphur tuft

© Nick Robinson

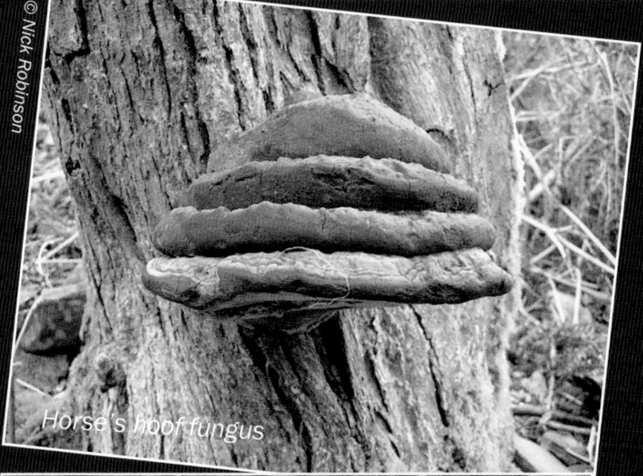

Horse's hoof fungus

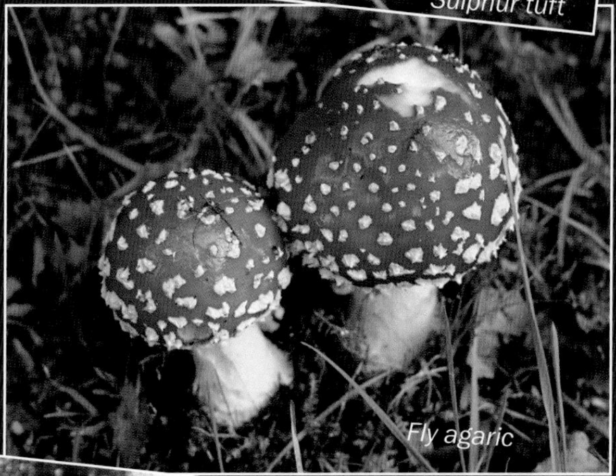

© Nick Robinson

Fly agaric

© Hilary Chambers

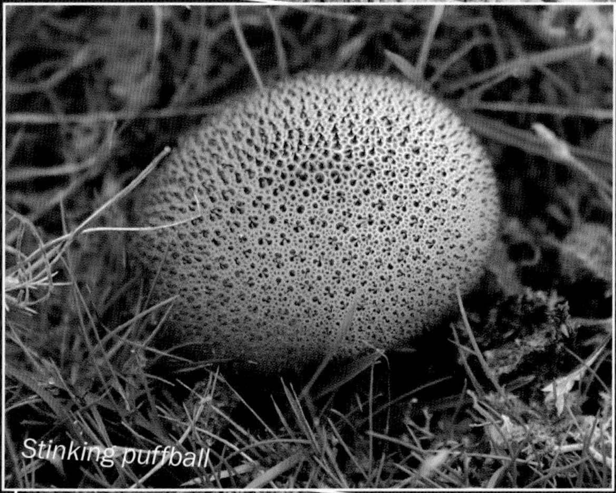

Stinking puffball

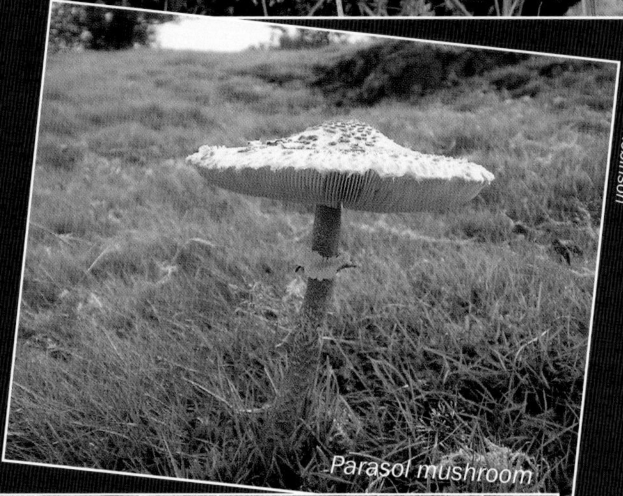

© Peter Carty

Parasol mushroom

© Nick Robinson

Golden waxcap

© David Evans

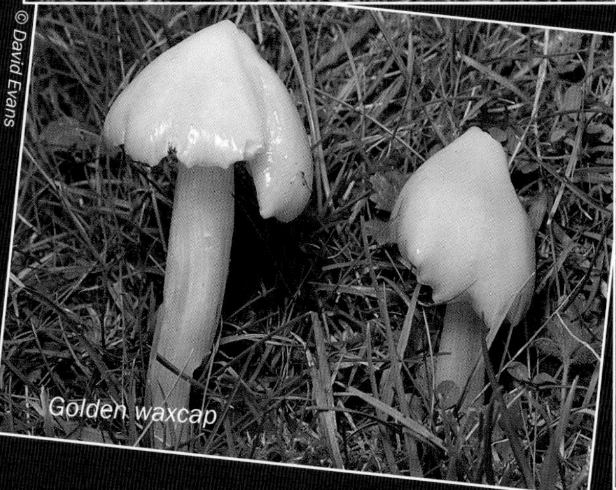

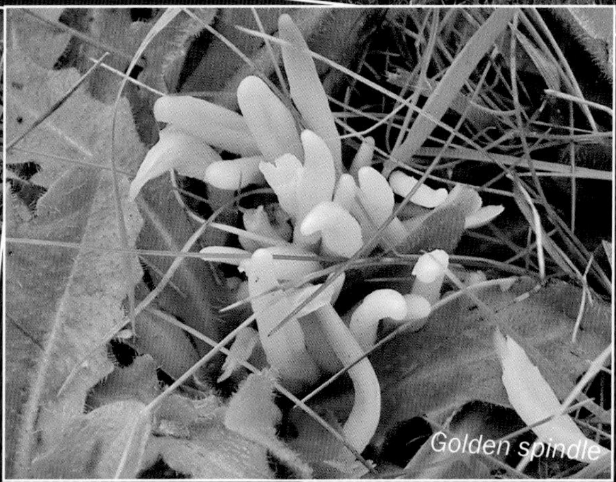

Golden spindle

November

Badgers do not hibernate but are much less active now though both badgers and foxes can been seen at any time. The population of smaller mammals, such as rabbits, shrews, mice and voles, drops dramatically during winter as food availability becomes the restricting factor to survival.

Winter is the time for the National Trust to survey the mature trees, fell those which are dangerous and cut logs for the wood-burning heating system in the Chalet and Tearooms.

HARD FROSTS may have started and early mornings are often misty as the dew from the ground condenses during the night. This month sees the last of the leaves on the deciduous trees falling to the ground. The only exception may be the beech which may hang on to its coppery coloured leaves and the larch with its yellow needles.

On the Long Mynd, sheep numbers are also reduced by the commoners to the agreed winter stocking levels to prevent damage to heather.

In the autumn nuthatches turn to the nut harvest for food, storing acorns, beechmast and hazelnuts by wedging them in cracks and behind the bark of mature trees.

December

THERE CAN be no mistaking that winter is finally upon us in December as frost grips the countryside and the trees are bare. It is from now until next spring that the battle for survival is at its most extreme for most animals as food is scarce and temperatures are low. There are a number of tactics to get through this lean period. One is to migrate to a warmer location, another is to stick it out on stored food reserves and what is still available, whilst another is to sleep it out (hibernate). Only dormice, hedgehogs and bats truly hibernate.

Teasel stems stand in clusters on road verges, where the ground has been disturbed and they have gained a foot hold. They are stark and brittle, their seed heads providing a favourite source of food for goldfinches who descend in 'charms' and twitter and fuss. Only small birds such as these, with slim and pointed beaks, can reach the seeds within the teasel head.

© Lee J Haywood

© Dan Pancamo

It is fun to follow the snow tracks of the inhabitants of the Long Mynd, to try to identify them, to see where they have come from and where they lead.

During the winter, the occasional hen harrier (female, illustrated) may be seen flying low over the plateau searching for an unwary meadow pipit, its favourite food. The male hen harrier is a pale bluish-grey colour with black wing tips. Short-eared owls may also be seen in the winter.

© Ann Middleton

Place Names

THE NAMES of places on and around the Long Mynd usually have a long and interesting history. Being so close to the border with Wales, it is not surprising that many of the local place-names have a Welsh origin. Indeed, Welsh was widely spoken as far east as Shrewsbury and Bewdley until the 18th century. The following lists some local place-names and their probable origin. [OE = Old English, ME = Middle English]

Asterton	*Easthampton*, eastern home farm
Batch	*baece*, land in a valley with stream (OE)
Burway	*burh* (fort) since the road passes one on Bodbury Hill
Butt	conspicuous hillock
Callow	*calu*, bare or bald (OE)
Coneygarth	*coning erth*, rabbit warren (ME)
Duckley Nap	*duck*, border + *ley*, clearing (OE) + *nap*, barrow or hillock
Gogbatch	*gogge*, bog (ME)
Haddon	*haeth*, heath or heather + *dun*, hill
High Park	*pearroc*, enclosed piece of land
Jinlye	*gin*, animal trap + *ley*, clearing
Mynd	(also Minton, Myndtown) *mynd*, (Welsh *mynndd*), mountain
Netebech	*neat*, cattle + *baece*, batch
Nover's Hill	*atten*, at (ME), *ofe*, 'at the flat topped hill'
Onny	*gwy* and *wy*, water (Welsh) or *onn*, ash trees (Welsh)
Picklescott	*Pikelescote*, Picel's cottage
Plush	(dialect) marshy
Pulverbatch	*puldra*, to gush (possibly Norwegian),
Portway	*porte*, town (OE)
Quinney	*gwyn*, white (Welsh) + *wy*, water (Welsh)
Ratlinghope	personal name *Rotel*, secluded place of the people of Rotel + *inga*, place in the valley
Stanyeld	*stan*, stone + *helde*, gentle slope = stony slope
Stretton	*stratun*, settlement on a Roman road (OE)
Synalds	*sid*, long (OE) + *hlaw*, hill (OE)
Wern	*gwern*, alder swamp (Welsh)
Woolstaston	*Ulestan*, personal name (OE) + *tun*, farmstead

THE FIRST detailed map of the Long Mynd was made in 1834 by Charles Mickleburgh. He labelled many of the hills and valleys with names which in many cases are quite different from the name by which they are known today.

Modern name	Old name on 1834 map
Ashes Hollow	Long Batch Gutter
Ashlet	Ashlight
Barrister's Batch	Wall Gutter
Breadhill Dale	Breadwell Dale
Burway Hill	Winter Hill
Calf Ridge	Calvocks
Callow Hollow stream	Rye Brook
Catbatch	Catch Batch
Dr Mott's Road stream	Black Gutter
Golf links, north end	Frinnage
Grindle	Catalls
Haddon Hill	Adons
Handless	Henllys
Knolls	Knowls
Lightspout, tributary above	Broad Withers
Minton Batch	Kinneys Batch
Minton Hill	Yapstone
Mount Gutter	Mount Hollow
New Pool Hollow	Cowridge Gutter
Small Batch	Little Batch
Townbrook Valley	Town's Brook
Yearlet	Earlitt
Batch west of Churchmoor Hill	Wooler Batch
Hill between Long Batch and Jonathan's Batch	Varnalls
Hill to the SE of the Finger post	Bran Knowles
Hill between New Pool Hollow and Devil's Mouth Hollow	Cunnary Bank

From other sources:

Town Brook	Black Valley (1900)
Carding Mill Valley	Mill Glen (1870)

Source References and Notes

1   Ordnance Survey Active GPS Network figure.

2   The Devil's Mouth is clearly marked on the 1834 Charles Mickleburgh and the 1883 25" OS maps; E S Cobbold, *Church Stretton*, vol 3, 1904, p54.

3   Mr Goodwin, the proprietor of the mill operated this drinks' business and an incident reported in the local newspaper (29 June 1899) records an accident involving the mill wheel. A young man showing off to a group of ladies, rested on the rail above and behind the wheel when he put his foot on the wheel. '...the upper troughs being full of water, the wheel revolved easier than he expected, the rail broke and he went head first over the wheel and became jammed'. Mr Goodwin and Mr Jones from Stretton House, managed to lever the wheel and freed the man. He was taken to the doctors' who was summoned from church. On examination he was found to have no bones broken. The man was left in no doubt that he was lucky not to have been crushed to death, admonished for interfering with other people's property and was put on the mail train back to Shrewsbury. Besides identifying the proprietor, this incident confirms the wheel to be still in operation at this date and *could* suggest that it is overshot contrary to all the written secondary sources noted so far. (Courtesy of Alan Brisbourne)

4   There is some confusion about when the mill ponds were constructed; they seem to have been rebuilt several times, presumably after failure of the dams. The 1837 tithe map shows two ponds in New Pool Hollow, none in Carding Mill Valley. The 1883 25" OS map shows one pond in Carding Mill Valley and two ponds in New Pool Hollow, the lower named 'Mill Pond' and the upper named 'New Pool'.

5   Sale notice 1870 (see page 130).

6   *Wellington Journal*, 22 May 1886 (Courtesy of Alan Brisbourne).

7   A postcard postmarked 4 Sep 1905 of the Carding Mill Valley shows the presence of the Chalet.

8   Indenture between 'Church Stretton Water Works Company Limited' and 'Church Stretton Water Works Company', dated 8 Nov 1900 re reservoir in 'Townbrook Hollow otherwise Black Valley'. Another mention of Black Valley is in reference 6 above.

9   *Shropshire Star* 24 Nov 2003.

10 Ronald Stevens, *Laggard*, 1953. (Courtesy of Mark Baigent)

11 *The Times*, 20 Nov 1947, p7.

12 *Victoria County History, Shropshire,* vol 10, p95.

13 *The Times*, 7 Feb 1865, p7.

Photo Credits

Index